P9-AFV-468

5-19-73
Pat Dever
Dan Dever
"
Thanks

THE SURVIVAL OF THE WISEST

By the same author: MAN UNFOLDING

THE SURVIVAL
OF THE WISEST

Jonas Salk

HARPER & ROW, PUBLISHERS

New York, Evanston, San Francisco, London

1817

THE SURVIVAL OF THE WISEST. Copyright © 1973 by Jonas Salk. All rights reserved. Printed in the United States of America. No part of this book may be used or reproduced in any manner whatsoever without written permission except in the case of brief quotations embodied in critical articles and reviews. For information address Harper & Row, Publishers, Inc., 10 East 53rd Street, New York, N.Y. 10022. Published simultaneously in Canada by Fitzhenry & Whiteside Limited, Toronto.

FIRST EDITION

Designed by Sidney Feinberg

Library of Congress Cataloging in Publication Data

Salk, Jonas Edward, 1914–
   The survival of the wisest.
   1. Man. 2. Philosophy of nature. 3. Wisdom. 4. Self (Philosophy)
5. Human evolution. I. Title
BD450.S26 1973   128   72-11875
ISBN 0-06-013738-X

To Françoise

who illuminates all of life

CONTENTS

INTRODUCTION
THE WISDOM OF NATURE

At a time when so much has been learned about Nature,* when the condition of Man is so full of seeming paradoxes, it is not surprising to find that many whose profession has been in the natural sciences† are now addressing themselves to questions about Man. Nor is it surprising that they do so in a way that reflects their background as well as their method of thought.

It is difficult, in such circumstances, for scientists to keep their minds on the subject matter of science‡ alone. The problems of Man affect the conditions in which scientists work as well as the events of personal, social, and political life. Therefore the interests of science and of many scientists are now not so far removed from the human context as when it was possible to be dedicated to the workings of science as

---

* By Nature is meant the universe, with all its phenomena.

† By the natural sciences is meant those sciences or branches of knowledge dealing with objects or processes observable in Nature, such as biology, physics, etc., as distinct from the abstract or theoretical sciences, such as mathematics, philosophy, etc., and those dealing with human behavior.

‡ By this is meant systematized knowledge in general.

if they were separable from the world of Man. The point to be made is that the human condition, altered by the evolution of science and scientists, has in turn so affected both that, perforce, their attention must turn increasingly to questions of general human concern.

Although science and the technology derived from it are seen by some as the "cause" of Man's current malaise, they may also be seen as an "effect" of a deeper cause, that is, the process of evolution itself, capable of being used to produce remedies not only through the application of technologic advances but by providing Man with a way of seeing himself from the viewpoint of the "wisdom of Nature." In this way wisdom in Man, which may be thought of as the natural understanding of "essence," "process," and "relationship" in life, human and nonhuman, might be augmented by the contributions of science to Man's knowledge of himself, as well as of the universe around him, which may be thought of as another effect of the development of science, different from that of technology.

Importance is attached to the notion that wisdom is of "practical value" for human survival and for the maintenance and enhancement of the quality of life. The hypothesis proposed and elaborated in this book is that Man can learn wisdom from Nature.

At times Man appears to react wisely, when he senses "too much" or "too little," even without "knowing" precisely to what he is reacting. We should pay heed to this phenomenon and try to understand it "scientifically."

I am convinced that, although we cannot predict the future, with understanding Man can, to a considerable degree, influence the course of coming events in his favor. This is based upon the evidence that a new transformation is occurring in the circumstances of human life—new in the history of Man and of the planet—to suggest that Man's past performance should not be taken as the *only* basis for judging his future.

Because of the inevitability of the evolutionary process, the present must be viewed from a perspective of the future, as well as of the past. From the past, we can learn in part *how to* and *how not to* conduct ourselves; and from imagining some of the elements which are likely to combine in shaping the future, we might learn how to behave not merely in terms of the past but in consideration of the effect of alternatives from which we might choose, based upon our knowledge of the "way," or the "wisdom," of Nature.

For almost two decades I have accumulated reflections and written papers or essays discussing such matters from this viewpoint, thoughts which arose as a result of my own experiences in medicine and biology. Some have been put together in a first book entitled *Man Unfolding*. The present book grew out of an idea that occurred to me in the spring of 1969 while preparing the Robert Kennedy Duncan Memorial Lecture to be delivered at the Mellon Institute of Carnegie-Mellon University on the value of science for man. A title that came to mind, half-seriously, was "Narcissism and Responsibility in Science and in Man." In the struggle to convert this into a lecture, a flood of ideas poured forth, more easily expressed in diagrams than in prose. The lecture itself was finally delivered with the aid of lantern slides to convey visually, in symbols, shapes and relationships of words, what could not be communicated by speech alone. The lecture, in effect, was seen as well as heard.

My purpose was to search for a natural explanation for the inversion in values occurring in our time. The ideas offered herein are an initial contribution to such an understanding, which hopefully will influence the movement of society toward improving the quality of life as well as survival.

October 1972
San Diego, California

THE SURVIVAL OF THE WISEST

I

A WAY
TO PERCEIVE

An unprecedented explosion of interest and movements concerned with the survival of the species is now taking place. The idea of the extermination, by Man, of various forms of life on the planet, and the danger to human life, induces a fear that preoccupies increasing numbers of individuals, especially of the generations now maturing. Those who are ecologically oriented and those who are profoundly concerned about the quality of life for the species as well as for the individual appear to stand in opposition to others less aware of such problems, who are more concerned with themselves in their own life spans. The fundamental difference between these two attitudes is that the first expresses concern for *the individual and the species*; the second reveals principally, and perhaps exclusively, an interest in the *individual* and the *particular group* of which he is a part. The more broadly concerned (i.e., *with the species and the individual*) fall into two categories. One consists of those born after such threats came into full evidence; the other, of those born earlier but who, having witnessed the change, are now

1

reacting to previously prophesied dangers which have become realities. Those preoccupied only with their own problems are either unaware or unperturbed in the face of a
process in human evolution to which others are sensitive and,
if aware, feel frustrated, helpless, or apathetic.

A major threat to the species is attributed to the increasing
size of the human population, which, in turn, is ascribed to
successes in science and technology. This "explanation" has
evoked an attack upon science and the exploitation of its
technology, to the development of which are attributed many
adverse effects upon the human species and upon other
forms of life. "Polluters" who befoul the planet affect the
"quality of life" and are regarded as a threat to the present
and future equilibrium of the species and of the planet. Those
who consider themselves *on the side of* Nature, and therefore
of the human species, see others in opposition to both Nature
and Man. Hence we are to be concerned not only with Man's
relationship to Nature but with Man's relationship to himself.

From an objective point of view and without arbitrary
reference to a presumed purposeful Being, we cannot establish the reality of the illusion that everything in Nature has a
preconceived or predesigned purpose, or project. This illusion
arises, in part, from the order that prevails in the universe,
and from the direction of evolution in the cosmos, with the
emergence of Man, capable of perceiving and examining the
process itself as we are trying to do.

We have the further illusion, in respect to living systems,
that Nature's "purpose" is the development of increasingly
complex forms and systems which are then selected for continued survival and/or evolution as experience proves their
value for such "ends" or "purposes." This definition, or description, fits the appearance of increasing complexity in the

course of the evolution of living systems in a process in which ends and means are inseparable and without finality—a process of "incomplete completion" in which the maintenance of "life," or of living systems, in evolution, is an end in itself.

The tenacity with which individuals and species "cling to life," reacting vigorously to the threat of its withdrawl, striving and contriving in every way possible, destructively as well as constructively, to continue to remain alive in spite of all opposition, has some of the manifestations of an "addiction." It is as if living forms possessed a property which, by definition, "demands" survival and evolution. Hence the illusion of "purpose" in Nature.

Man possesses an additional characteristic, which has to do with the satisfaction and fulfillment of larger desires, which are concerned with the maintenance of the quality of life. This tendency may be subsumed under the term "sense of aesthetics," which, as used here, should be understood in its broad meaning as an "intuition of beauty and order." This aptitude, increased by desire, has the quality of an "addiction." Man is caught in all these processes without as yet realizing that this sense "demands" that he devise and exercise "naturalistic"* forms of "regulation" and "control" to protect himself from madness and from autodestruction. His concerns, thus far, have been more with details than with the overall picture. He has been occupied with disease and death, and with the amenities of life appropriate to each age and epoch. He has not yet seen the importance of understanding *life's* "*purpose*," and, therefore, *his purpose* individually and collectively, and of understanding where he fits into the evolutionary scheme of things. When he does, he will then better comprehend his own nature and develop ways and means of

---

* By this is meant imitating Nature.

dealing with the problems of life *as part* of the process of life itself, not as questions to be avoided or obliterated.

Viewed in this way we realize how much blindness to Man's true nature actually exists. This may be understandable in the young, who have not lived very long, but it is equally true of those who have lived longer. How we grapple with our blindness is of the greatest importance for the present and the future; it is the central problem of our time.

If human life is to express as much harmony, constructiveness, and creativity as are possible for fulfilling the purpose *of* life, as "required" by Nature, and the purposes *in* life, as "chosen" by Man, an attitude will be needed, not of Man "against" Nature, but of Man "inclusive with" Nature. A more reasonable attitude would be for Man to "serve Nature" in order to serve himself, rather than to "serve himself" without regard for, or at the expense of, Nature and others. By recognizing and respecting the natural "hierarchies of purpose" Man would be better able to gauge his latitude to select and pursue his own "chosen purposes" without coming into conflict with the "purpose of Nature," which appears to be the continuation of life as long as conditions on the planet permit.

As a process, evolution seems to be Nature's way of finding means for extending the persistence of life on earth. This involves the elaboration of increasingly complex mechanisms for problem-solving and adaptation. The ability of the human mind to solve the problem of survival is part of this process. In this respect Man has evolved so successfully that he is now to be tested for his capacity to "invent" appropriate means to limit the harmful or lethal excesses of which he is capable. The conflict in the human realm is now between "self-expression" and "self-restraint" *within* the individual, as the effect of cultural evolutionary processes has reduced external restraint upon individual expression and increased opportunities for choice.

The fork-in-the-road at which Man *now* stands offers either a path toward the development of ways and means for maximizing self-expression *and* self-restraint, by means of external restraints that are not suppressive or oppressive, or an alternative path of limitless license which would unleash destructive and pathological greed at the expense of constructive and creative individuals. In the latter case, a strong reaction can be expected to develop in response to the sense of order upon which their survival is based. The challenge is to establish an equilibrium between *self-expression with self-restraint* on the one hand and *self-protection with self-restriction* on the other.

If Man is to take advantage of opportunities to remedy difficulties that have arisen as a result of his evolution, then he needs to understand his relationship to the evolutionary process which plays with and upon him. At this point in time hypothetical models of probable patterns and mechanisms involved would have to be tested for validity and would be helpful for guidance.

As we sharpen our ability to discern the pattern of order that must exist in the seeming chaos that we wish to comprehend, as we distinguish the elements that compose the conflicts and paradoxes of our lives, we encounter striking differences between age-groups in the questions, preoccupations, and values espoused, especially in the so-called advanced countries. This is most marked in the U.S.A., but by no means restricted to it; there is ample evidence of the same phenomena in other areas of the world where similar circumstances and conditions have developed. The observations with which we are concerned are not intended to be reflective of the U.S.A. alone, but rather of the nature of Man as it may be deduced from human behavior under the influence of changes that have occurred in very recent times.

The multiplicity of factors and causes operative in the human realm makes it exceedingly difficult to discern the nature of ordering principles without oversimplification. Nevertheless, the process through which Man is now going and the striking differences in behaviorisms among men—some of which are quite paradoxical—call for a way of perceiving that might allow understanding of the otherwise incomprehensible.

II

THE SIGMOID
CURVE

As a logical overture, in our search for models, let us look at a curve describing the growth of the human population on the face of the earth and the present reasonable projection over the next few decades to the year 2000 (Figure 1). This curve tells the story simply, although within it are expressed vast and complex implications for the character and quality of human life which concern relationships as well as resources for the present and the future. The trajectory not yet traced raises questions as to the means that Man or Nature will invoke to deal with the excesses that have developed and the insufficiencies that persist. Will Man create his own procedures to deal with them or will Nature's simple ways come into play, some of which may prove quite undesirable from Man's point of veiw? This, in fact, may already be occurring.

Before turning our attention to the questions and consequences of the rapidly mounting curve of population increase as drawn in Figure 2, or to the implications of its curtailment or of its continuation, let us look at patterns of growth in

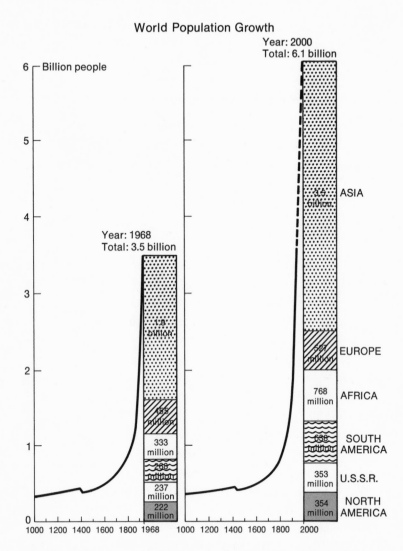

Figure 1. Population by world areas A.D. 1000-2000. From *World Facts and Trends.* Copyright © 1972 by John McHale, published by the Macmillan Publishing Co., Inc.

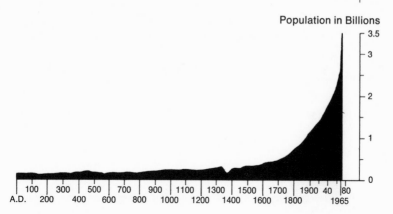

Figure 2. World population estimates, A.D. 0-1965. Adapted from *World Facts and Trends,* by John McHale.

other living systems. For example, Figure 3 shows the growth curve of a fruit-fly population in a closed system as observed by Raymond Pearl in 1925.

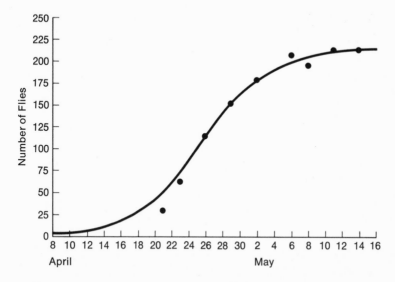

Figure 3. Growth of fruit-fly population. From *The Biology of Population Growth,* by Raymond Pearl. Copyright 1925 by A. A. Knopf, Inc. and renewed 1953 by Maude de Witt Pearl. Reprinted by permission of the publisher.

Population Growth of Yeast Cells in Culture

Time (hours)	Population Size (number of individuals)	Growth Rate (individuals per hour)
0	10	0
2	29	9.5
4	71	21
6	175	52
8	351	88
10	513	81
12	594	40.5
14	641	23.5
16	656	7.5
18	662	3

Source: Adapted from Raymond Pearl, *The Biology of Population Growth,* A.A. Knopf, Inc., 1925.

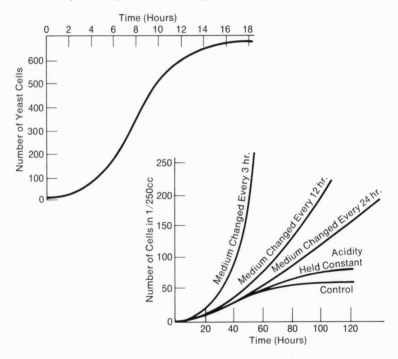

Figure 4. The upper graph depicts the growth curve of yeast cells grown in a laboratory culture and refers to the table immediately above. The lower graph shows the growth curves of yeast cells grown under varying environmental conditions. From CRM Books, *Biology: An Appreciation of Life.* © 1972 by Communications Research Machines, Inc.

The S-shaped, or sigmoid, curve which describes the growth of fruit flies is also seen in curves of growth of microorganisms (Figure 4) and of cells or molecules. For example, the curve describing the production of antibody molecules after "vaccine" injection is shown in Figures 5 & 6. Similar

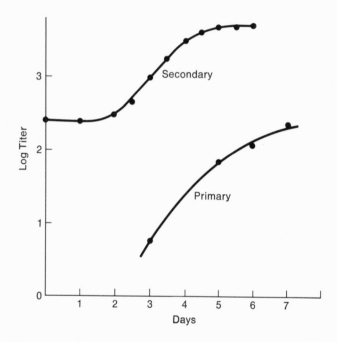

Figure 5. The primary and secondary antibody responses of two rabbits to intravenous injections of a "vaccine." From F. M. Burnet and Frank Fenner, *The Production of Antibodies,* published by Macmillan and Company Limited, Melbourne, 1949.

curves are seen for hormone production after suitable stimulation, and a similar effect occurs in tissue repair after injury. Significantly, this is *not* true in cancerous conditions, where the cancerous cells have escaped the normally present control and regulatory factors which have developed in the

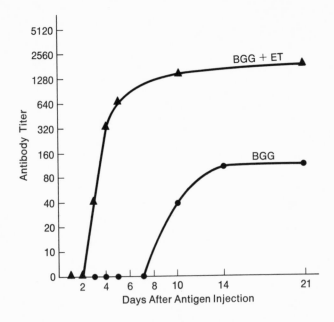

Figure 6. Primary antibody response in mice injected with bovine gamma globulin (BGG) with and without the reinforcing effect of another substance, endotoxin (ET). From Maurice Landy and Werner Braun, *Bacterial Endotoxins,* published by the Rutgers University Press, 1964.

course of evolution in surviving organisms. Since the planet earth can be considered a closed system and *since the sigmoid curve reflects the operation of control and regulatory mechanisms which appear to be associated with survival of the individual or of the species* it would seem reasonable to expect that the pattern of future population growth in Man will tend to stabilize at an optimal level described by an S-shaped curve as in Figure 7a. It is possible, of course, that an alternative pattern might resemble that of the lemmings (Figure 7b), in which periodic catastrophe occurs with enormous loss of life. However, Man's attitude toward human

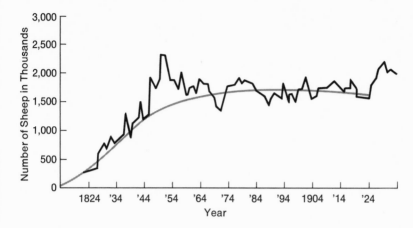

Figure 7a. Growth curve of sheep following their introduction to an area. Note initial sigmoid pattern followed by approximate equilibrium.

life would have to alter significantly for such patterns to be endured; he is more likely to choose *other ways than catastrophe for maintaining optimal numbers on the face of the earth while remaining within the limit of available resources.*

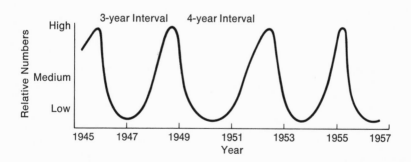

Figure 7b. Generalized curve of the three-to-four-year cycle of the brown lemming population. From CRM Books, *Biology: An Appreciation of Life,* © 1972 by Communications Research Machines, Inc.

As Man has still to complete a cycle of growth on this planet, he has not yet fully revealed the pattern biologically programmed in him, or the way it will be influenced by factors he is responsible for, or by natural forces beyond his control. Therefore we are unable to know the pattern of his trajectory in the short- or longer-term future. The "catastrophists" and harbingers of doom *are in themselves evidence that Man possesses a signaling mechanism for sounding warnings* of danger, sensed more acutely and more clearly by some who alarmingly represent the problem of population increase as shown in Figure 8.

If we assume, however, that Man has the power of choice and can influence the course of his growth curve on this planet, then it is of special interest to look carefully at the

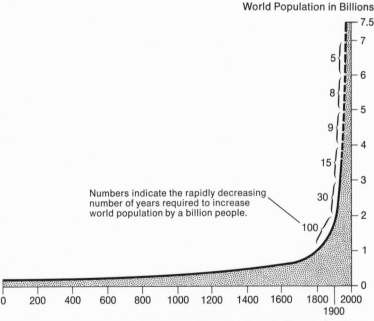

Figure 8. Adapted from "The Population Bomb" by Paul R. Ehrlich, © 1970 by The New York Times Company. Reprinted by permission.

sigmoid curve in terms meaningful for him. Since our deeper purpose is to try to discern the nature of order in the human realm in relation to the nature of order in the realm of life in general, it is interesting to explore the possible meaning of the similarities observed in the human population growth curve as manifested thus far, and the first portion of the growth curve of the fruit-fly population and similar curves in the subsystems of other living systems.

Since, through the process of natural selection, living organisms which have survived have revealed their fitness for persistence thus far in the evolutionary scheme, we would like to have some prevision of Man's program. Is he programmed for relatively short-term survival in which his end may come of his own doing? Or is he programmed for a life in which only those who have lost the power to discriminate, or who are otherwise degenerate, will continue to inhabit the planet as long as reproductive activity continues to supply "victims" of life, struggling to preserve itself in the "human" form? And what other alternatives exist?

It is likely that Man's brain has developed as it has, in the course of natural selection, partly in response to exogenous forces active against survival. Does that same brain also possess the capacity to tame and discipline those inner forces which act against long-term survival, in opposition to a life of high quality? The struggle for survival once manifest principally *between Man and Nature now seems to be taking place within the human species itself, between Man and men* and within the individual himself.

My purpose is to elucidate the factors and forces affecting the quality of human life through ideas which emerge while "playing with" the growth curve and reflecting upon the developmental and evolutionary processes of Man in the critical stage in which we seem to be at this point in time.

III

WHAT HAPPENS
AT THE POINT
OF INFLECTION?

I𝖥 𝖶𝖤 𝖠𝖫𝖫𝖮𝖶 our imaginations free rein to reflect on the implications for Man of the curve depicted in Figure 3, which represents the fruit fly's population growth, and if we think in anthropomorphic terms, assuming the flies are sentient beings possessing foresight and insight, then it is apparent that the "outlook" of each new generation must differ from that of others depending on the circumstances prevailing at the point in time along the curve when that generation came on the scene. As we study the curve in Figure 9, consideration of the lower portion only gives the impression of continuous, even explosive expansion, whereas consideration of the upper portion gives the impression of modulation and control of this expansion, so that finally a limit is established. At the junction of the lower and upper portions of the curve is a region of inflection at which there is a change *from progressive acceleration to progressive deceleration* and at which the influence of the controlling processes is clearly visible. The break apparent in this region suggests that a "signaling"

16

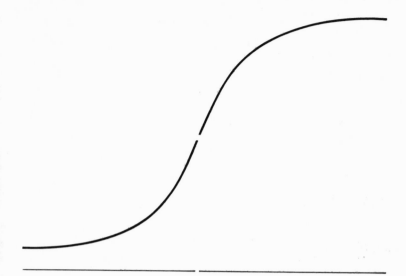

Figure 9

mechanism of some kind must operate to bring about this change, producing an effect which, judging from the shape of the curve, indicates the existence of a uniform process, reflecting the operation of some kind of ordering principle in response to "signals" both from the environment and from within the organisms themselves. At different points in time along the curve, latent qualities and reactions are evoked appropriate to survival, the program for which is coded in the germ plasm, which also contains an accumulation of control and regulatory factors essential thereto.

At the plateau stage of numbers, the individuals in the fly population would be expected to "behave" differently as compared with those alive earlier in the growth curve, i.e., before the zone of inflection when different "problems" prevailed. The extent to which circumstances differ, at different points in time along the curve, is graphically suggested in

Figure 10 by breaking the continuity at the point of inflection so as to create two curves, A and B.

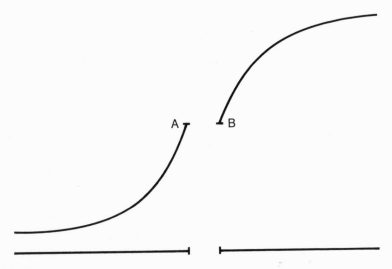

Figure 10

These curves are intended to emphasize the difference in attitude and outlook in the two periods and help create a visual image of what can be sensed "intuitively." They also convey concretely what might be appreciated "cognitively" by means of an objective analysis of the increasingly complex problems generated by the growing numbers of individuals. In the discussion to follow, curves A and B will be used as symbols of the "shape" of the past and of the future, as we attempt to characterize each. When we speak of the fruit fly in anthropomorphic terms, it is to suggest, using this caricature, the nature of the forces operating in the human realm. For example, if we speak of the flies as possessing, individually or collectively, a "sense of responsibility" and "insight and foresight," it is to suggest the existence of the equivalent of conflicting forces by which they would, were they human, be impelled to "judge" and "choose." Such judgment would be exercised according to the contesting "value systems" that would be in operation during periods as different as those suggested by curves A and B.

The fact that the fruit flies are a product of a long evolutionary history, whose survivors react according to their genetic programming, leads us to think that Man, who is of more recent origin and, moreover, at or near the point of inflection in his present curve of population growth on the planet, is about to find out whether he is programmed to behave in ways leading to a population growth curve similar to the fruit fly's, or to a curve of another shape. He has still to find out about the nature of the quality of life under circumstances which remain to be experienced. In being tested for survival, he still has a way to go not only quantitatively but qualitatively. The curves, however, provide some insight, their shapes suggesting the character of the problems that prevailed in the past, those now existing, and those likely to be encountered as Man continues to move through evolutionary time.

Man differs from other living organisms in possessing another "control and regulatory" system, for response to environmental and other changes, in addition to that genetically coded and automatically operative as in the fruit fly, which has been tested and selected in the course of its evolutionary history. Man is able to exercise learned behavior. He also possesses individual will, which can be either in accord or in conflict with genetically coded patterns of response. In this sense Man is more complex and more unpredictable than the fruit fly. He can learn to behave in ways that are anti-life as well as pro-life, anti-evolution as well as pro-evolution. He remains to be tested for this pattern of response to all that is implied in the need for changing values to make the transition from Epoch A to Epoch B. In view of the greed and ideologies of Man as causes of his conflicts, attitudes as well as values will be put to test in the transition from Epoch A to Epoch B.

Genetic programming does not change as rapidly as the attitudes and values that also guide human behavior. Since genetically as well as culturally determined responses are "environmentally" linked, the circumstantial differences implied by the dissimilar "shapes" of the curves symbolizing Epoch A and Epoch B will be expected to evoke different sets of genetic as well as cultural potentialities. In Epoch B those attitudes and attributes which are of the greatest value will determine the "real" and not merely the "presumed" shape of the population growth curve and the quality of life. Value systems such as prevailed in Epoch A will, of necessity, have to be replaced by those appropriate for Epoch B, and new concepts will emerge about the nature of Man and his relationship to all parts of the cosmos. Since the conditions into which future generations will be born are not yet determined, it will be of interest to see how men in different cultures, with different genetic backgrounds and capacities, will respond to the human and planetary changes now well under way. It is not yet possible to see how Man will deal with attributes which dominated in Epoch A nor to foresee very clearly precisely what attributes will emerge in Epoch B.

Thus Man is being subjected to a new and possibly more severe challenge than ever before, for which he needs perspective and insight. He must become aware of the opportunities and the dangers that he will have to face when confronted by the conflicts resulting from a necessary inversion of such magnitude as implied by the diagram in Figure 11. The profundity of the change in values required for

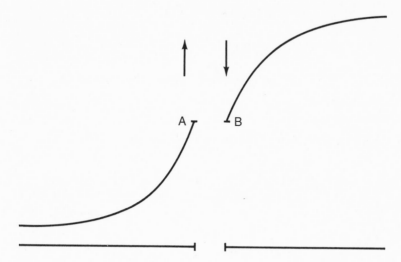

Figure 11

survival and for quality of life in the periods described by curves A and B makes it seem not only that what was of positive value in A may, in fact, become of negative value in B; but also, if "B values" had prevailed earlier they would have been of opposite value in the A epoch. From this point of view it is not difficult to understand the depth and meaning of the change which Man is now experiencing in the various forms that have already become manifest under the specific historical circumstances in different cultures in all parts of the world.

IV

CONFLICT
IN VALUES

In foreseeing a future as radically different from the past as suggested by the shapes of curves A and B, Man would be expected to react in a manner appropriate to the changing circumstances and altering inner patterns which arise in the course of his own growth and development. To the extent that he is aware of this, sufficiently evolved, and able to so act, in the new epoch he will make choices and live his life thereby in relation to a sense of the future in Epoch B different from the future of Epoch A, because of the changes implied by the difference in the shape of the curve.

We speculate that the inversion in values which we have just referred to is a natural accompaniment to the transition associated with the point of inflection in the human population growth curve. It suggests the existence in Man of the capacity to behave in accordance with more than one value system and that the trends which dominate are influenced, in part, by the aggregate of the prevailing conditions and circumstances that also affect the evolutionary process. Man's adaptability and his capacity to choose play an important part in this process. An overt struggle over values is becoming evident, tending toward a shift in dominance between two basically different systems that have long coexisted as two parts of a conflicting dualism. This situation is diagrammed in Figure 12 by the lines which are shown to cross

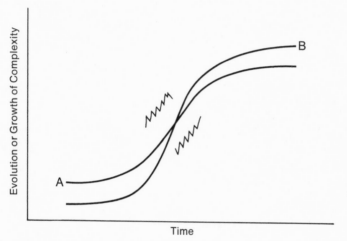

Figure 12

and change position relative to each other at the inflection point; one line is designated A and the other B—each referring to the relative position of the conflicting sets of values and characteristics as a function of time. This suggests that the A and B values and characteristics coexisted and grew separately and yet together, until circumstances caused B to accelerate or otherwise find greater expression, or A to slow or otherwise be arrested.

The details of the processes involved may be summarized as due to the interaction of a variety of biological and cultural factors, causing increasing complexity with a multiplication of processes, leading to further growth, development, and evolution to an optimal level in a dynamic equilibrium the maintenance of which is also influenced by changing environmental factors.

However, it is obvious that Man is basically a dualistic system of inborn and learned responses. That individuals differ in their behavior is well known, and our newly acquired understanding that certain behavior characteristics are transmitted genetically, makes it seem likely that genetic factors also have a determining effect upon patterns of thinking, of reactivity to different circumstances in life, and to the influence of others—whether in the early days, weeks, months, or years of life. Thus innate as well as acquired patterns have profound effects upon prevalent modes of behavior which reflect not only the nature of the circumstances of life, and especially the effects of early influences, but also the intrinsic nature of the particular individual. Nevertheless, the major shifts observed are due, in more limited degree, to biological change or hybridization than to what might be called cultural "hybridization," which has been markedly facilitated and accelerated by greater ease in communication and transportation, and increased educational opportunities. Together, they have augmented intermingling and developed talent that would otherwise have remained latent.

If we were to characterize some of the differences in attitude and concern believed to be due to a "generation gap," we would observe that the younger generation rebukes the older for what it regards as hypocrisy and for espousing certain values which it rejects, while the older rebukes the younger for certain of its values and behavior. The extremes of each group attack the other with the greatest violence. Whatever conflagrations result are due to a greater degree of divergence of the extremes than of the means, which are less different, and which move toward each other with greater ease and grace. Therefore, as we describe differences, it is to be borne in mind that they do not characterize in any absolute way those native to each epoch, but rather the predominant tendency toward an "exclusive" "*either/or*" attitude—which does not allow any common ground with members of the other group —as compared to an "inclusive" "*and*" attitude. "*Either/or*" attitudes characterize those who remain outside the moving blended curves of growth and development which includes past, present, and future.

The extremist views may be described by drawing curves A and B in relation to each other, as in Figure 13, in a way

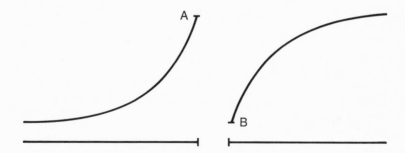

Figure 13

demonstrating that each group does not conceive the inflection in values occurring as evolutionary. One group perceives only negative value in the past, from which it wishes to dissociate itself, as well as from the rest of the world—as if it were possible to establish an existence which did not grow naturally out of what had gone before. The other extreme cannot conceive of the inevitability of the change that is taking place and regards it as something to be opposed rather than guided. These exaggerations suggest that individuals obviously have different perceptions of themselves and of others, and the breadth or narrowness of their cosmologic view influences their attitudes and their behavior. Some react as if returning to Nature—living off the earth or as part of a small commune—were the desired state. The values and conduct of others are adapted to a world capable of indefinite growth and change as suggested by an undeflected projection of Curve A. Some see error and some see evil in the preceding periods and act as if all vestiges of the past should be eradicated and a new beginning be made, as if it were possible to disregard the billions of people who have gone before and who now exist dependent upon their life-support systems and accustomed ways of life.

Figure 14 reveals the pattern of perturbations that con-

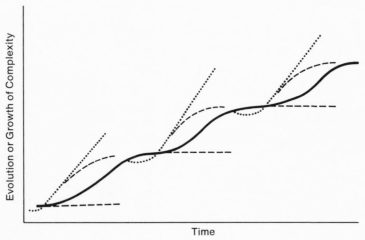

Figure 14

tinually occur in the cultural evolutionary process, which proceeds dialectically just as evolution does in the living universe. That which survives, of that which is new, is not only the "fittest," but that which "fits best" in the constantly changing circumstances. Even though small, perturbations are cumulative in their effect and thereby reach the limits of tolerance of the system. Periods of rapid change are followed by quiescent intervals, until an innovation appears which once again disturbs the equilibrium and gives rise to a further step in the process of evolution toward higher and higher complexity.

Figure 14 renders schematically three sequential periods of change. The lines that move upward and to the right represent those who contribute, or agree to, change; the horizontal lines projecting to the right represent those who counter, or resist, change. Such trends give the shape to the sequence of curves. For simplicity, the trend lines are shown on the diagram only at the plateau stage when the effect of initiative, innovation, and inertia is most evident. Similarly, when the rate of change is the greatest, some individuals, the most active in espousing change, join and are joined by those from the mainstream, while others maintain their relatively extreme positions. These individuals continue to move in a direction that does not become part of the evolutionary scheme of things and might even be judged to be anti-evolutionary. Such extremes often represent nonfits, or misfits. They usually continue as passionate as before, while the change that has occurred is of such dimensions as to leave them way out on the limb of the cultural evolutionary tree.

The dip below the horizontal, in the line that moves upward and to the right, reflects the fate of "dropouts," who may be impelled for all the right reasons (as suggested by the trends realized later in evolution) but who may not survive, perhaps because the attempt was premature or because their attempt was a necessary prelude to what was to follow. The volume of the mainstream is then swelled by the resisters and the advocates of change. In each "generation," "new" events arise which may be selected, thus contributing to the cultural evolution of Man. This is similar to the changes seen in biological evolution, with the selection of mutations resulting in changing patterns altered by the character of those "selected" for survival.

The perturbations shown in Figure 14, in the aggregate and over the time scale of Man's evolutionary history, are the cause of the effects observed in Figure 2 (page 9). These, therefore, are the results of a large number of greater and lesser events. In this way Man has reached a point, occurring in our time, when an epochal change is being experienced. This change is of such magnitude and significance that it may well be judged to be of major import in the course of human evolution. At this time Man seems to be seeking tolerable levels quantitatively and is being called upon to develop qualitatively satisfying ways and means for living with himself and with others that fit what might be thought of as the scheme of Nature. Man's choices will be "judged" by Nature, thus revealing the wisdom of his selections from among many alternatives.

The purpose of this work is, in part, to discern Nature's "game," as well as Man's. The choices which Man makes from the alternatives available to him will profoundly influence his own evolutionary destiny. The outcome will reveal the extent to which he will have succeeded in understanding the workings of Nature, at a time in his own evolution when he is being tested for his capacity to accommodate himself to change, and for his ability to create the possibilities for existence under circumstances as different from those of the past as suggested by the shapes of curves A and B. Until this point in evolutionary time Man has been selected for characteristics that were of value for survival during the A epoch. Now, quite abruptly, a new "selection pressure" has appeared, for which he is ill-prepared by experience but for which there may exist within him a reservoir of potential appropriate to the new circumstances such as are now developing.

In the course of evolution many more species have become extinct than have survived, each perhaps for particular causes very different from those which might cause the extinction of Man. For in Man's case, at this point in his evolution, his extinction might well arise for internal reasons. The way he deals with unresolved conflicts within himself individually and collectively might lead to his own destruction. The process of natural selection has developed survivors resistant to various infectious diseases and to some of the vicissitudes of the environment. It has also led to the selection for survival of those successful in escaping the ravages of war and those ingenious enough to escape human tyranny. Thus until now the qualities that have been selected for survival reflect the conditions and circumstances that have prevailed as much as the potentialities that exist in Man. As Nature continues its game of biological mutation and selection, and as Man plays his own games of selection of ideas and of cultural innovations, Nature will have the last word. Therefore it is up to Man to look closely and deeply into Nature's workings, not only at the molecular and cellular levels but also at the consequences of advancing knowledge and cultural practices as these bear on the question of survival and the quality of life. It is in this respect that wisdom will be required for which a balanced creative center for judgment is needed.

We must look to those among us who are in closest touch with the unfathomable source of creativity in the human species for an understanding of the workings of Nature and for insight into Nature's "game," as we enter upon an epoch in which new values are required for choices of immediate need as well as for those with longer-range implications. This is especially important when, as now, the number born in each new generation exceeds the number born in each of the earlier generations. For this reason, the character and quality of the individual which will survive and predominate in our period will have a very profound effect upon the character and quality of human life for a long time to come.

To what extent will we be able to affect the course of Nature, in the short or in the long run? That remains to be seen. Nevertheless, we are fully conscious of this problem. How will we deal with this opportunity and this responsibility knowing as much as we do? What more do we need to know, being as aware as we are now of our limitations and our capabilities?

V

BIOLOGIC ANALOGUES
OF THE BEING
AND THE EGO

In the first chapter the idea of a balance between Man's self-expression and self-restraint was introduced. Since Man is here conceived as composed of BEING and EGO, the BEING both expressed and restrained by the EGO, it will be necessary to define and examine these terms which will occupy a central position in the discussion to follow.

The BEING, defined as absolute existence in a complete or perfect state, lacking no essential characteristic, appears at the moment of fertilization, possessing the surviving essence of its forebears as well as its own individuality. *It is not conceived as located in any particular structure or part of the brain, although its existence and expression depend upon the physical structure in general and the brain in particular.* Its existence is evident only through the effects it produces.

The BEING of Man is the center in which exist the possibilities which when unfolded reveal the essence of the person both as a member of the species and as an individual. It contains the undeveloped patterns of behavior, as expressed in work, which, when evoked by circumstances, opportuni-

31

ties, and choices, express the potential contained therein. The characteristics of the BEING are hidden until revealed in the course of life's experiences. Thus it can be developed or not, depending, in part, upon awareness of its existence and knowledge of the factors required for its cultivation and expression. *Consciousness of one's own* BEING, *in this sense, is a prerequisite to full self-development as well as to full self-expression with self-restraint;* the word "self-discipline" means, at one and the same time, *expression with restraint.*

If the BEING of Man is meaningfully related to what might be thought of as Nature's "purpose," its essential character must be discovered through its own expression, guiding the means it possesses for so doing while, at the same time, influencing the circumstances of its existence and evolution which are revealed by the effects "caused" by it.

The BEING cannot be easily circumscribed, yet objective evidence of its existence is manifest in the behavior and works of Man as well as in Man's thoughts and feelings. The BEING acts according to the laws of Nature and, existing by virtue of these laws, takes on a reality that is not easily dismissed even though its precise structure and chemistry cannot be defined.

In order to comprehend its nature, its relationships, development and functions, and to understand the kinds of malformation and malfunctioning which can affect it, an analogy might be helpful. The analogy that comes to mind is that of the genetic code, or message. BEING, when realized, corresponds to the genetic message, which, when decoded, reveals the organism programmed therein. Although here thought of as an analogue of the genetic code, the program of the BEING and of the elements necessary for its development and expression, or for its restraint, are also inscribed therein.

If BEING is analogous to the genetic code, then the EGO, by which we mean the enduring and conscious element that knows experience, reacts to the outside world, and thus mediates between the BEING and the demands of the social and physical environment, would be analogous to the somatic system in its relation to the genetic. Thus the relationship between BEING and EGO is perceived to be similar to that which exists between the genetic and somatic systems. If the latter are complementary and *inter*dependent parts of a unit, then, by extension of the analogy, the BEING and the EGO are similarly related. Since the genetic system contains the program for the possibilities of the organism, and the somatic system the structures and mechanisms necessary for its expression, then the BEING would contain its program and the EGO would afford the means necessary for its expression. Just as the existence of the somatic system depends upon the genetic, the reverse is also true. Somatic structures provide the ways through which the genetic program is expressed and related to other parts of the organism and to the environment, both internal and external; the EGO, by analogy, would be the tool of the BEING, communicating with it, with others, and with the environment, by many different modalities.

Just as the somatic system, if malformed or malfunctioning for any reason whatever, can constitute a limiting or inhibiting influence upon the genetic system, so the EGO can be in conflict with the BEING or, if developmentally impaired by external or internal factors, can adversely affect its expression. If the somatic system serves some "program" other than its own proper genetic system, as, for example, in the presence of a virus capable either of cell destruction or of cancerous transformation, then the "integrity" of the whole unit composed of genetic and somatic elements, in a complementary relationship, is affected. Similarly, and ideally, the EGO should serve the BEING as the somatic system should, ideally, serve its genetic system, which protects, expresses, and perpetuates both the genetic and somatic systems of the individual and the species. If, however, the EGO comes under the influence of other EGOS, so as to alter the "program" in a way that would not serve its own BEING, but rather some "other" EGO, a potentially destructive effect is possible, as in the case of the cell-destroying or cancer-inducing viruses referred to above; however, the possibility also exists for a potentially "advantageous effect" which could be measured in terms of survival advantages, as in the instance of the viruses responsible for the variety of colors in tulips or the bacterial virus responsible for toxin production in the diphtheria bacillus. The relationship we imagine between the BEING and the EGO bears a great number of resemblances to that existing between the genetic and somatic systems.

VI

THE PHYSICAL,
THE BIOLOGICAL,
AND THE METABIOLOGICAL

To HELP CLARIFY our understanding, in evolutionary terms, of the nature of Man's BEING and EGO, for better comprehension of his behavior, an analogy has been drawn between the genetic-somatic dualism and the BEING-EGO dualism. Before developing this further, the nature of the genetic and somatic systems and their relationship should be explained in more detail.

The material of which the genetic system is composed performs a twofold function: (1) in *germ cells* (i.e., egg and sperm cells) that of passing information on to the next generation through the role it plays in perpetuation of the species; (2) in *somatic cells* (i.e., all other differentiated cells of the body) that of controlling and regulating the function of each of the cells of the organism in its particular role in the organism as a whole. Somatic material (the function of which will be seen below) is also contained in cells of the germ plasm (i.e., cells involved in perpetuation of the species) and cells of the somatoplasm (i.e., all other cells of the body). One of the distinctions we are trying to make when we speak of genetic material and somatic material is between "species substance" and "individual substance," both of which are present in all cells of the organism.

The germ cells, upon fertilization, form another individual consisting of germ cells, capable of repeating and, therefore, perpetuating this process, and of somatic cells, which also serve a purpose in survival and evolution. Through new generations of individuals the process is maintained as long as the species either survives in its existing form or is changed as a result of mutation and natural selection.

Genetic material consists essentially of DNA molecules, which, in germ cells, carry hereditary instructions from one generation to the next and, in somatic cells, form a material of which the principal components are RNA and protein molecules so organized as to reproduce genetic *and* somatic substance. While the genetic material of each germ cell contains the program, or plan, for replicating the entire organism, the genetic material of somatic cells contains the same program, in a modified state, for forming and carrying out the particular function of each specialized cell. The program for the formation of somatic material is contained in the genetic material. The somatic substance, in turn, functions in constructing genetic material, as, for example, through the enzymes, programmed in the genes, which are necessary in constructing the genetic substance itself. This kind of relationship reveals and emphasizes the nature and extent of the *inter*dependence of the two separate systems. Together, these are the essential elements of the basic pattern of the cells of the organism, of the organism as a whole, and of all species which are related in that the nucleic acids and proteins of which they are composed are constructed of the same building blocks. They, in turn, are made of the chemical elements which are formed of elementary particles found in the non-animate material of the physical universe.

With the proposed conception of the roles of the BEING and EGO and their relationship, it is of interest to explore the role of the EGO in the expression and satisfaction of the BEING. We commonly call this self-expression and self-satisfaction. From the analogy to the genetic and somatic systems, the EGO system is conceived of as serving to facilitate self-development and self-expression; this requires the exercise of measured self-restraint and self-discipline. The EGO may also exercise unmeasured restraint or discipline, thereby reducing its value in the development and expression of the BEING, even to the extent, at times, of having a negative effect.

A parallel to this is seen in the malfunctioning of the somatic constituents of a cell acting upon the expression of its genetic potentiality, under the influence, for example, of an RNA virus. This leads to failure of development, and therefore functional failure, not only of the cell but of the organism of which it is a part. These manifestations are seen in cancerous transformation as well as in "abnormal" cell metabolism and in dying cells. There are other examples, such as the "nonstimulation" or "nonchallenge" of cells or of systems which leads to failure in developing somatic possibilities, expressing the genetic potential, the organism thereby failing to reveal its genetically latent possibilities. The result is an excessively restricted behavior, eventually without usefulness; many different factors produce such effects in cellular and organ systems.

It is necessary to study in detail how the EGO is formed and how it functions relative to the BEING, both in the course of development and later in life. Also to be studied is the effect of prevalent ideas and of patterns of social behavior upon the BEING-EGO relationship.

The BEING is conceived as containing and defining the limits of the individual's "capability," the EGO as possessing the power to influence either its full development and expression, or its premature constriction, or incomplete evolution. Thus the power of the EGO in relation to the BEING can have a positive or a negative influence. In much the same way, the EGO, in turn, is influenced and shaped by others' EGOS. Thus, in the interactions that occur in the course of life, the BEING, laid down "by Nature," interacts with its own original, or "instinctive," EGO with which it was first endowed, which, in turn, interacts with the "environment." Progressively, the "native" EGO responds to many outside influences, including the EGO influences of others. Thus the BEING, which is "immutable," can be influenced by the effect of the EGO upon its expression, suppression, or nonexpression. BEING can also be destroyed by the atrophy of nonstimulation, or by exhaustion due to "frustration." Thus the BEING and the EGO, although distinct, are interdependent; the maldevelopment or malfunction of either results in behavioral "disorders."

The BEING and EGO of Man have here been defined by comparison and analogy with the genetic and somatic systems. We will henceforth refer to "BEING-EGO" phenomena as "metabiologic" to distinguish them from those that are more closely and more obviously related to the "genetic-somatic" level of "biologic" organization.

The physical basis of biological processes is now well understood. Their structure-function relationships are clear, as are many of the general laws governing them. Our new need is to comprehend the relationshp between structure and function in metabiologic processes and their connection to the biologic. Furthermore, as the biology of the central nervous system begins to be understood, including the specific function and role of different parts of the brain, comprehension of the mind of Man, which is seen, in part at least, as a metabiologic phenomenon, can be developed from a more solid base.

By thinking in terms of metabiology, and by distinguishing BEING and EGO factors, then the principles or laws governing their function may begin to become apparent. At least this will provide a basis for study and discussion of certain of the uniquely human manifestations for which, without a common point of reference, many different terms are now used. Such expressions as the "Biology of the Spirit" used by Edmund Sinnott, the term "transcendence," and others with similar connotations need to be examined from a common point of view, as can be done by juxtaposing what is here called the metabiological and the biological. Thus some of the uniquely human phenomena which we are calling metabiological, and which have appeared in the course of evolution, can begin to be understood using biological models for description and for study.

Just as the evolution of concepts, first in the physicochemical and then in the biological realms, depends upon the ordering and organizing effect of a "scientific" approach, and just as the laws and principles of physics and chemistry proved useful for understanding the structure and function of living material, insights will be sought as to the nature of metabiological processes by comparison with, and analogy to, the biological.

Since the word "metabiology" is new, and is as yet to be defined, an attempt is made in Figure 15 to give it meaning relative to other branches of inquiry. One question that

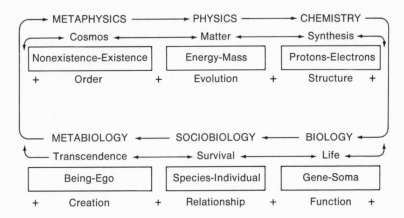

Figure 15

naturally arises is that of the relationship between the terms "metaphysics" and "metabiology." In the sense that the word "metabiology" is intended to mean "beyond biology," metaphysics does not mean "beyond physics." The word "metaphysics" came into use as a result of the title supposedly given by the Alexandrian librarians to the work in which Aristotle treats the problem of the first philosophy; the word was used to signify "the books which came *after* the books on physics." Since neither the substance nor the scope of metaphysics is agreed upon by all, it is necessary to say that in Figure 15 the meaning intended is that it is the branch of philosophy that treats of first principles and is concerned with the nature of existence, or being, as such. It deals with the origin and general structure of the universe, with all its parts, elements, and laws, and with the inquiry into the origin, nature, methods, and limits of human knowledge. The other terms used in Figure 15 are more familiar and are also defined according to the nature of the questions with which each is concerned.

As stated in Figure 15, with diagrammatic oversimplicity, metaphysics is concerned with the Cosmos; physics with matter; chemistry with the synthesis of matter; biology with life, or with living matter which arose by synthesis from physical matter; sociobiology with survival of complex forms of life; and metabiology with transcendence, or going beyond the ordinary limits of living matter, i.e., surpassing or exceeding the biological. The phenomenon of transcendence is seen as an effect of the existence of the BEING-EGO dualism; art, science, and other forms of human creativity are among the many ways in which this is manifest. Order arose from the first, or original, dualism, which was nonexistence-existence. Evolution began with the energy-mass dualism, which then gave rise to the proton-electron dualism. The latter formed structures which continued in synthesis with the appearance of the genetic-somatic pair in complementary functional relationship. With further evolution, more highly complex relationships formed and the species-individual dialectic arose. Finally, the BEING-EGO dualism emerged with the appearance of Man. Each of these dualisms is perceived to be analogous, and for this reason they are shown in similar blocks in the diagram. The arrows indicate the order of complexity of subject matter, from metaphysics to metabiology, and their interrelationship. Whatever eventually appears in the course of evolution must be implicit in whatever pre-existed; and all that exists contains the essence of the elements from which they evolved. Order, if dynamic, implies evolution of structure, function, relationship, and creation. Creation, in turn, implies the existence of order, evolution, structure, function, relationship.

In the foregoing scheme, living matter is regarded as having arisen as a "mutational" event in the course of physicochemical evolution; living matter then continued to evolve with increasing complexity, and as a "mutational" event metabiologic phenomena appeared. "Mutations" of a meta-biological nature continue to be expressed in the effects produced by the mind of Man and this is seen as part of the evolutionary process itself. For the sake of completeness, we can think of the process of evolution as beginning with the origin of physical matter. This can be imagined as the "first" or the "original mutation." This question is a proper one for metaphysics; however, the process by which this could occur constitutes a problem for physics.

These notions are offered to reveal a way of thinking about the diversity manifest in the physical and living universe which has arisen in the course of evolution to the continuity of which Man is actively contributing.

VII

MUTATIONS

THE ORDER SEEN in Nature also exists in biological processes; therefore ordering principles that operate in the metabiological realm must also be sought. Metabiologically as well as biologically, evolution occurs through a variety of mechanisms, involving "mutation" and "selection." "Mutation" implies the spontaneous appearance of new inheritable information resulting in new combinations which are then tested for evolutionary value in the course of experience. "Selection" implies preference according to the prevailing criteria of biological and/or metabiological values.

Biologists have discovered many ways in Nature of acquiring such information and of producing new combinations. For example, sexual reproduction, which results in new mixtures of inheritable information, may be seen as a producer of "mutations" in the sense implied above. "Mutations," as here defined, would also be produced by the introduction, either naturally or experimentally, of a virus into a sperm or egg cell, the genetic information of which would then be incorporated in either the DNA or the RNA and transmitted.

Such new information might be advantageous or disadvantageous. Nevertheless, it would be transmitted hereditarily, having become part of the organism, whose survival value would then be tested in the process of natural selection. Other ways of altering inheritable information are by the application of X-rays to germinal tissue, or by chemical means; these effects are mediated by DNA or RNA alterations. Purely accidental errors, or copying errors, in the course of gene replication, or of protein synthesis, produce similar effects. In all instances the survival value of the products for continued evolution are determined subsequently.

Similarly, in the metabiological realm, new perceptions arise from time to time, which occur spontaneously, or by deliberate search. These have effects analogous in a way to new inheritable biological information in its transmissibility from generation to generation by cultural means. New perceptions can also be spread, as would the hypothetical virus proposed above, to alter, favorably or unfavorably, the behavior of the individual arising in this way, those related to him, as well as those to follow. In the metabiological realm revolutionary ideas may be seen as part of the process of evolution, equivalent to the occurrence of "mutations" in the biological domain; they are then subjected to the process of "selection for survival" to be retained until changed or eliminated.

Founders of religions, prophets, and political leaders have formulated many different concepts and systems to guide human life. Some have been the product of imagination, without basis in "reality." Some of those who, in the past, constructed imagery by which Man could live with his BEING and with others may have spoken poetically rather than

literally. Although they have served to help Man through
critical moments in evolution, providing a conceptual frame-
work by which to live, as knowledge of reality has advanced,
poetic formulations have continued to be regarded too literally or not metaphorically enough.

Human imagination furnishes Man's emerging consciousness with means for perceiving the forces which he senses
but to which he is otherwise blind. Thus consciousness has
been expanding rapidly through validation of what some
envisioned earlier, or had observed and interpreted differently and in ways contrary to later knowledge and beliefs.
Through this process, Man has come to the threshold of a
state of consciousness, regarding his nature and his relationship to the Cosmos, in terms that reflect "reality." By using
the processes of Nature as metaphor, to describe the forces
by which it operates upon and within Man, we come as close
to describing "reality" as we can within the limits of our
comprehension. Men will be very uneven in their capacity
for such understanding, which, naturally, differs for different
ages and cultures, and develops and changes in the course
of time. For these reasons it will always be necessary to use
metaphor and myth to provide "comprehensible" guides to
living. In this way Man's imagination *and* intellect play vital
roles in his survival and evolution.

As we come closer to comprehending the nature of the
universe, and of Man's relationship to the Cosmos and to his
BEING, metaphor and analogy will also be useful as tools for
seeking comprehension, and for finding the interrelatedness
of Truths and the relationship between Truth and Beauty.
Metaphor and analogy are means to expand and refine consciousness to express what is known, in ways suitable to
minds at different levels of development so that the same

meaning may be understood by all. In this way it is possible to communicate even between those widely separated in age, culture, or metabiologic development. This will become increasingly necessary, as time goes on, to allow the extension of the process of "intertwining" and "coalescence" toward the formation of an organism of mankind and not merely a collection of coexisting units acting more competitively and destructively than constructively. The idea that Man's aggression is expressed only destructively, or largely so, must be re-examined in the light of the evidence that aggression is also constructively involved in creative work, and in all activity useful to the person himself and to others.

Consciousness can be expressed in a wide variety of ways; reality can be seen not only by the minds of scientists but by the minds of artists, each using his own means for perceiving as well as expressing. By artists we mean poets, playwrights, novelists, people who convey by metaphor what the scientist tries to express explicitly of the nature of the universe he studies. The artist and philosopher deal, by and large, with what we have been speaking of as the metabiological universe. We are now seeking the connection, or the relationship, between the biologic and the metabiologic.

VIII

A NEW KIND OF
HUMAN ANIMAL

THE PURPOSE of introducing into this discussion such terms and ideas as BEING, EGO, and metabiology is due to my belief that a major cause of the "special" revolution now taking place in some parts of the world—made manifest particularly in the United States—is the result of a change in the relationship of the BEING and the EGO, as well as a basic modification in their character, illustrated in the changes observed in currently prevailing human values and behavior. These changes are as real as many other human manifestations of the past and are taking new and different forms which have a special and perhaps different meaning than previous ones. They bear evidence of continued growth, development, and evolution in a process that is by no means near its end. On the contrary, the present stage may be looked upon as a kind of new beginning: old laws, rules, or values are no longer considered adequate, and a whole new system of relationships, values, and rules needs to be developed and accepted as more appropriate to the presently changing circumstances.

The nature of the occurring transition is suggested by the diagrams that have been drawn in an attempt to convey the character of the process through which Man is evolving metabiologically. These diagrams afford useful mental images of the pattern of the process, even if they do not provide the details to test their validity for different systems, circumstances, and relationships. They convey the nature of the trajectory of Man into the future in terms of numbers, and this has many qualitative implications. They also show that former attitudes in respect to growth in population can no longer continue. Now self-imposed restrictions of freedom in this respect will be necessary not only to preserve other freedoms but to keep the quality of life from falling to a level that would soon become intolerable.

Qualitative factors that are acceptable to some are intolerable to others, often constituting a cause of disagreement, dissatisfaction, and conflict, not only with others but with one's own BEING. For this reason, attention must be focused upon the BEING and the EGO and their role in the life of Man. As mentioned earlier, even though the physical location of the BEING and EGO may never be identifiable, these terms, nevertheless, do refer to phenomena that are recognizable both by their subjective and their objective effects.

The original intent of this book was to draw attention to the role of value systems as control and regulatory factors which operate in an apparently "intuitive" way, guiding Man toward or away from survival. We have arrived at a point of realization that the evolutionary process, in moving inexorably toward higher and higher complexity, has resulted in the appearance of metabiological phenomena, including the BEING and EGO dualism. In these as in other inextricable dualisms in Nature, problems of balance exist in relation to a "natural" order. It is according to such order that survival and evolutionary potential are maintained, and that which survives is that which fits best for survival *and* for evolution, under circumstances that also evolve in a constant interplay of distinct but *inter*dependent forces and processes. The perpetually creative nature of evolution is manifest not only in the myriad specimens of the physical and the biological universe but also in the human, or metabiological, worlds. The BEING and the EGO are also varied in their separate, combined, and resultant effects and have now come strongly to the fore, demanding deeper and more detailed understanding intrinsically as well as in relationship to each other and in the relationship of Man to men and of Man to the Cosmos.

Keeping in mind the analogy that has been drawn with the genetic and somatic systems, the BEING is seen to consist of a set of patterns for "behavior-structure" formation that are evoked or educed under appropriate circumstances. Early in life a large multiplicity of possibilities exists—each of different quality and intensity. As time goes on, the capacity and power for development and expression diminish and are eventually lost. Only those possibilities which had been educed and exercised will have come into existence and will persist as long as they are sustained by need and use. Unexpressed patterns might persist to be revealed later, under appropriate conditions, if relevant skills exist. The patterns of the BEING are thought of as the equivalent of a genetic code representing the accumulation of patterns of responsiveness that arose by mutation and "internal" selection followed by natural, or "external," selection. Thus, as Man has continued to evolve and more and more individuals have tended to survive, protected by artificial or "man-made" support, more varied patterns of capability have accumulated, selected by various *rites du passage* or other cultural, environmental, or social influences.

Concurrently with survival, the removal of cultural, environmental, and social restraints caused a new kind of "human animal" to appear in larger numbers; problems were of a different character because of differences in the nature and relationship of the BEING and the EGO. One effect of the increase in numbers has been to reveal the enormous heterogeneity in respect to BEING and EGO patterns as well as in values, purpose, and self-discipline in dealing with Man's desires and needs. Thus, superimposed on the biological attributes of Man are the metabiological attributes which also constitute an important area of human biology for which understanding is so urgently necessary.

What emerges from all of this is the existence of two basic types of programs, with two sets of purpose, intrinsically and inextricably interrelated. The EGO program, for example, is related to survival in the present; the BEING program, to fulfillment of some destiny not altogether discernible. Ideally, as in the genetic-somatic dualism, they are complementary programs, neither competitive nor mutually exclusive. They are complex and varied, and unless they function together and simultaneously, lead to imbalances calling for correction. These complementary dualisms constitute the elements of life, providing the basis for order and balance in survival and in evolution. They exemplify Nature's dualisms, which are part of the fabric of existence.

Thus existence by definition includes two basically related patterns and programs which cannot be at war with each other but rather must coexist in healthy tension, each contributing its part to the process of being and becoming in a game of evolution for which there is no knowable end in the course of existence, and which can always end in nonexistence. Thus during life the problems that are posed are of being and becoming, of which survival and evolution are two examples illustrating two types of programs of which we must be conscious in human existence.

Complementary programs can be related cooperatively or competitively, constructively or destructively, for or against survival and evolution. As has been pointed out, functional disengagement of one from the other, or dominance of the EGO over the BEING, or of the somatic over the genetic, will lead eventually to serious impairment of both and to eventual extinction. The cooperation of these two factors leads to their enhancement in processes that augment the joint state of being and becoming. It results in a fullness of health not only of the biological but of the metabiological systems and processes.

The essential point here made is that healthy* existence bespeaks an attitude of *and* between the components of complementary dualisms rather than an attitude of *either/or*, which gives rise to an unhealthy existence and, if not corrected, leads, eventually, to nonexistence. This implies a distinction between healthy antagonism and unhealthy antagonism and suggests that "hierarchy" in living systems serves to reduce antagonism in higher and higher forms of complexity; resolution of conflict between complementary elements by inclusion in a hierarchy of more complex purpose leads to further evolution, whereas resolution by competitive "elimination" has a contrary effect. The latter is useful when applied to "anti-evolutionary" patterns, or to "anti-evolutionary" resolutions, which must be extirpated as enemies of the

* By health is meant an ordered dynamic equilibrium in the processes of growth, development, and evolution.

evolutionary process itself. However, so long as evolution continues and natural selection operates, distinctions and choices will be made for those factors favoring evolution against those that do not. The former will survive; the latter will not.

There is an economy of effort and energy in the natural selection process which tends to a choice of the best with a minimum of means; this, in turn, provides another basis for evaluating alternatives. Such value judgments, and the mechanisms for making them, are an intrinsic attribute of Nature and the basis of order in living systems and the human realm. However, there is, at times, a tendency on the part of Man to make "economy" of sole importance and to minimize or deprecate other qualities necessary for maintaining the "diversity" upon which evolution is also based. Thus arises the need to recognize *both* diversity *and* economy, and not one to the disadvantage or detriment of the other.

We have learned about orders of biologic complexity; we now need to learn about metabiologic complexity. The former are guarded and expressed genetically and somatically; the latter by the BEING and the EGO. These, in turn, are revealed implicitly in value systems and operating mechanisms and are more explicitly expressed in terms of "hierarchies of purpose" for establishing priorities of goals, and "hierarchies of position or status" in groups or in society for executing the many functions involved. "Purpose," in this sense, is analogous to code, whether genetic (and therefore biologic) or to the essence of the BEING (and hence metabiologic); "position or status" is thought of as analogous to somatic structures, biologically, and to the EGO, metabiologically. Purpose refers to order and program, and position or status to the protecting and executing function for expressing the program and maintaining the integrity of the order. Both sets need to work harmoniously, as must the dual elements of any complementary system. When position or status in metabiologic systems becomes disengaged from purpose, and an end in itself, it tends to resist evolution or change, and destruction is invited as a function of the evolutionary process itself, leading to nonsurvival and nonexistence.

Thus *existence* implies continued evolution, or change, as well as continued survival; it means not only the "survival of the fittest" but the "survival of that which fits best" in the evolutionary scheme of things. Purpose as well as status changes relative to the needs for survival and for evolution. Since survival is a prerequisite for evolution to proceed, and since evolution is essential for increasing the probability for survival, existence depends upon the establishment of patterns of order relevant to a dynamic evolutionary process. Thus for Man the processes of survival and of evolution separately and together require judgments for continued existence that, in time, will prove to have been wise.

When we speak of the survival of the wisest, by wisest we mean those who comprehend the survival-evolutionary process, as well as the being-becoming process, and who make choices such as enhance the possibility of existence rather than nonexistence, recognizing evolution as an essential and inexorable continuum of growth and development.

To pursue this theme, the next chapter will be concerned with other dualisms in which relationships are changing on the eve of the new phase designated as Epoch B. We have anticipated the next chapters by creating the expectation that a change is occurring in the patterns of order and values in Epoch B as compared to those of Epoch A, which we will now examine in more detail.

IX

BEYOND COEXISTENCE:
THE NEED FOR BALANCED
COALESCENCE

THE IDEAS CONTAINED in the foregoing chapters were
developed after we considered biological and human behavior as the resultant of the operation of dual agendas in
the biological and metabiological realms. Success in dealing
with any problem is based upon the unconscious or conscious recognition and appreciation of the two complementary components of each dualism in a balanced coalescence.
Mere cooperation or coexistence, although necessary, is not
sufficient, since this implies "independence" but not necessar-
ily "*inter*dependence." "Cooperation" or "coexistence" could
become "competition," with a tendency toward a "win-lose"
resolution for "dominance." This kind of game and outcome
is untenable between elements of such complementary dualisms as those to which we have been referring. These required coalescence for persisting as part of the evolutionary
process, implying the need for "double-win" rather than
"win-lose," or, at least, "nontotal loss" by either element. The
latter implies that something must be gained by *both* elements of the complementarity even if it is only continued
existence, or continued survival in the evolutionary scheme of

things. This is illustrated by the nature of the relationship between Life and Death, for example, where total win by either would result in total loss for *both* since without Life Death could not exist and without Death neither could Life. The impossibility of dominance of one over the other may be seen to have been obviated through a "double-win" resolution with Life "winning control of the species" and Death "winning control of the individual," in which these two independent systems, which operate according to different sets of "values," and hence different "agendas," are indissolubly "*inter*dependent."

Man has long been inventing and testing systems for dealing with the problem of "dual agendas" such as exist in the relationship between BEING and EGO, between individuals and the species, and between Nature and himself. However, he is now confronted by the fact that this is a world-wide problem affecting all areas of the earth and all population groups. The necessity to deal with it on so large a scale arises at a time when he possesses not only a vast human reservoir of experience but a knowledge of living systems which can suggest new ways of looking at old unsolved problems. In so doing, he may even discern how to anticipate or avoid problems.

Man possesses foresight and a capacity to imagine and to relate seemingly unconnected events. Although artists, poets, and those engaged in "creative" work are thought to be especially endowed with those qualities, many others also have such attributes. If more individuals become sufficiently evolved in this respect, they will be capable of further development so as to be more sensitively responsive individually and to each other, resulting in increased empathy and augmenting "coalescence."

However, the effect of EGO factors, and EGO-mediated influences, upon the BEING, and the existence of incompatible EGO structures among individuals, make it difficult to know the BEING of Man in its "native" state, unaffected by the circumstances of life. Pure "BEING" is nonexistent; the BEING is manifest through the EGO system, however adequate or appropriate. Although the EGO is largely shaped by postnatal influences, in part it is also genetically determined. Because of the extent to which experiences in life play a role in EGO formation and in EGO function, it is necessary to understand the conditions and circumstances for EGO development which are most conducive to the fulfillment of the potential of the newborn BEING. It is as important to establish this as to understand the nutritional factors necessary to build healthy bodies and to know the diseases that can be prevented to avoid crippling or premature death.

The principal underlying idea is that the BEING and EGO of Man are as important for the development and maintenance of a healthy balance in the organism as, for example, the sympathetic and parasympathetic nervous systems, the musculature and the bones, and all the other complementary systems of the body. Just as each of these plays an important role in survival and evolution, so do the BEING and EGO of Man. It is postulated that they are also actively involved in what is occurring in the course of the transition from Epoch A to Epoch B.

Even with his capacity for consciousness, Man is driven largely by forces to which he is blind. The time has come to study his BEING and EGO systems, his metabiology, with the same kind of discipline as that with which biologists have examined the genetic and somatic systems of all forms of life. The use of the genetic-somatic analogy for the BEING-EGO systems provides a way of comparing "human" value systems in terms of "natural" value systems and of looking at Man and at life from the viewpoint not of "good" and "evil," in terms of "man-made" moralities, but rather of "natural relationships" based upon the scheme of things in evolution. This is different from the present way of looking at Man and could have an enlightening effect upon our existence, allowing us to develop in Epoch B in a way that was not possible in Epoch A. The prospect of an entirely new approach to the future could provide a greater measure of incentive and hope than one based merely upon attempting to correct the past and adapting it for a qualitatively different future.

If the character of the days to come were to be determined by different sets of values, this would imply a morality and an ethic different from those shaped and imposed primarily for the purpose of "group" preservation, which often fought against the equally strong inherent tendency in Man to preserve, express, and unfold the BEING of the "individual." Thus, in the past, the "survival of the fittest" among individuals and groups called for strong EGO elements on the basis of which individual survival was established and preserved. Now it appears as if survival will favor EGO patterns that are not ends in themselves but rather serve the BEING without dominating it. The new trend that appears to be developing is toward greater cooperation, and even coalescence, among "like" persons, i.e., persons in whom BEING-EGO are compatible in purpose and means; the "object" of their relationship being to bring out the best in each other. Such relationships would have greater value for producing feelings of satisfaction and fulfillment in Man and, therefore, would tend to be favored if human choice operated through an EGO system developed to serve the BEING.

In an attempt to present some of these ideas graphically,

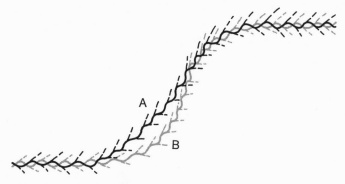

Figure 16. The form and design of the curves are similar to those shown in Figures 12 and 14. This graphic method of conveying an idea and its implications are discussed in the text.

the diagrams in Figures 16 and 17 were drawn. The A-curve and the B-curve can be seen as referring to EGO-dominated and BEING-dominated individuals, respectively. The diagrams suggest that an effective complementary interrelationship existed early in human evolution and, in time, a separation developed between the two, with control of the EGO-dominant over the BEING-dominant. In Figure 16 an optimistic view of the future is depicted by the intertwining lines suggesting a renewed complementary interrelationship between EGO and BEING. Instead of seeing curves A and B as describing the EGO-BEING relationship, they may also be seen as depicting the influence of intellect (A) and intuition (B), of reason (A) and feeling (B), of objectivity (A) and subjectivity (B).

The implication of the difference between Figures 16 and 17 is that the character of the future will depend upon whether or not a successful complementary relationship is effected between BEING and EGO, intuition and intellect, and other similarly complementary dualisms. The separation of the A and B lines in Figure 17 is intended to convey the idea that the development of EGO-dominated individuals, with insufficient BEING development, who overpower those who are BEING-dominant can lead to a different outcome from that depicted in Figure 16.

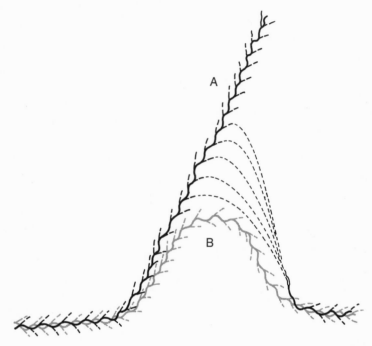

Figure 17. See legend to Figure 16.

Whether the factors symbolized by the lines do intertwine, as suggested in Figure 16, or do not, as in Figure 17, will be determined in the future, as will the consequence of one course or another. Different rates of growth of two interrelated patterns, or structures, or sets of forces in a single entity would be expected with time to create stresses under the changing conditions or circumstances which affect them.

A simple physical image as to how this occurs is that of two fused metals, each with a different coefficient of expansion with changing temperature. The principle involved is used in thermoregulation. If the dual elements in the many processes of life are visualized in this way, it is not difficult to see how bends occur, giving a sigmoid shape to self-regulating population growth curves, when built-in forces arise to reverse the trend and to effect equilibrium and balance at new levels. The diagrams suggest similar effects in living systems, in which there are the equivalent of two bands, or two sets, of forces, as suggested above. These would tend to remain together as the two elements reacted alternately to each other, producing "intertwining" effects. Each band is visualized as trending either toward or away from the apposite band. Another image is that of a growing double helix, which would look like the self-replicating DNA molecule.

The diagrams help us become aware of Man's position and role in the evolutionary process of which he is a part. First, he is an object in a process of Nature; second, he has been exercising his highly developed creativity and will, which appeared in the course of his metabiological evolution with striking effects upon him and with irreversible consequences on the face of the earth.

The diagrams provide a way of viewing the components in the complexity of human life, that we cannot perceive as easily without reference to a simplified and, in a way, abstract image of the basic pattern of relationships in actively evolving living systems. By the use of a pair of interrelated sigmoid curves, and by assigning the word "BEING" to one and the word "EGO" to the other, we are able to see the changing relationships, through time, between these two distinct but *inter*dependent parts of Man which undergo development separately and together in a mutually related process. Through the use of a visual model, a symbol is created which becomes a common way of seeing relationships in conflict and in harmony—of understanding the basis for agreement and disagreement, constructiveness and destructiveness, health and pathology.

The concept of the distinct, yet *inter*dependent BEING and EGO and the importance of their separate, yet related and simultaneous development suggest that we need to study the biology of these two systems, including their genetics and the effect upon their development of internal and external influences. This implies that BEING patterns as well as EGO capabilities are inherited and that cultural factors constitute the equivalent of an environmental force which provides the opportunity for, and influences the character of, their expression, just as environmental influences are needed to reveal genetic capacity in biological systems. An example given elsewhere is that of a bacterium which requires the presence of the sugar that is to be digested to initiate the induction of the digesting enzyme, provided the organism possesses the genetic capacity to so react. The activation of EGO capabilities can be likened to this.

Such studies could lead to understanding the great variety seen among humans, comparable to that seen among species of plants and animals. Human varieties might eventually be classifiable according to types of patterns of perceiving and thinking, for example, and would account not only for the different manifestations of talent and skills but for the reinforcing or inhibiting effects seen among individuals of different types. The absence of striking "physical" differences as correlates of such types hides the existence of differences in "patterns of perceiving and thinking." By "patterns of perceiving and thinking" is also meant "patterns of dreams" that arise in the BEING and are translated by the EGO system into forms that can be variously expressed and communicated, as in works of art, of invention, of attempts to establish a logical basis for comprehension, or in the many other ways manifest in Man.

My aim here is to suggest that the tendency toward the separation and isolation of human groups according to EGO values that have formed and prevailed until now has prevented the recognition and expression of the BEING. They have favored the association of individuals according to EGO values rather than BEING values. If, as is suspected from what has been happening in the human realm, BEING standards are emerging with EGO values appropriate thereto, removing the encumbrance of essentially foreign EGO values which contributed to the development of enormous internal and external conflicts, then Man is entering upon a new phase of his evolutionary development. It can lead him to unforeseeable possibilities and also to unexpected problems. For whatever success may be possible, and whatever danger is to be avoided, it will be necessary to understand, in more detail and in depth, the intrinsic nature of the BEING and EGO systems, the ways in which they are manifest, and to find ways and means of becoming increasingly conscious of what we still so largely fail to comprehend.

X

TO DISTINGUISH
THE WHOLESOME
FROM THE SICK

It would be very pleasant, indeed, if it were unnecessary to occupy ourselves with the "pathological" and the destructive, and to be concerned only with the "healthy" and the constructive. But that would be as unrealistic as trying to see life in general, and human life in particular, only from an "optimistic" point of view. If we are to recognize and choose those alternatives, or options, with value for survival and evolution, it will be necessary to recognize and to distinguish between the "wholesome" and the "sick," as seen from a developmental and evolutionary point of view. *There is a high degree of dynamic relativity in living Nature, and what may be regarded as healthy under one set of circumstances may be unhealthy under another.*

Since the laws of Nature have a bearing on human survival and fulfillment, we must try to recognize the tendencies that operate *against* the development of a dynamic equilibrium. If Man were as "wise" as Nature in respect to evolutionary survival, he might then be able to act accordingly to such tendencies in himself; this would imply knowledge and wisdom not only of "Outer" Nature, of which he is a part, but of his "Inner" Nature.

It appears as if individually and collectively Man possesses "responsibility," and "accountability" for the choices he makes affecting his own life, his species, and life in general on this planet. If exercised wisely, such responsibility would ensure the prolongation of his own presence as an individual and as a species, under circumstances maximizing human satisfaction and fulfillment. He has exhibited his power to counter disease, and, to some extent, death as well. He has also shown his power to create unhealthy conditions on a vast scale and to bring about death generally as well as selectively. Now, however, it is within his reach to alter the shape of his curve of growth, and the existence of a great many living systems, including his own. As he extends his influence, trying, for example, to alter the growth of cancerous tissue, and even to control his fertility, will he—as he learns, with even greater refinement, to control death and birth—use this power wisely for advancing physiological health and economic well-being and for reducing disease and suffering in the psychosocial realm? Such power could as well result, however, in diminished satisfaction and fulfillment and in an increase rather than in a reduction in suffering, causing the development of a more intolerable state for the human BEING and the body that houses it.

Since "adversity" for the individual is, in fact, part of the evolutionary process, which, by definition, implies dealing with adversity and is, therefore, essential for its maintenance, it will be important to compensate constructively for eliminating the difficulties of life which Man is designed to overcome; such needs are more often seen retrospectively than in advance. Thus there are both danger and reward to be mindful of in the steps Man takes toward improving his condition.

Having referred to duality in Nature generally, using as an example the coexistence of life and death as well as of health and disease, it should be clear that Man exists in a state of balance between life and death, between health and disease. He is called upon constantly to maintain equilibrium and to increase the margin, so as to remain in the zone of health, and as far from death as possible for as long as he can. He is free to use, in many other ways, the knowledge and wisdom he has acquired in the course of so doing. He may do so to improve the quality of life, as well as to reduce the incidence of disease.

So far as Man is concerned, it would seem therefore that the acquisition of knowledge and wisdom constitutes a purpose that could be of evolutionary value and therefore might be expected "to be looked upon with favor" by Nature. If we are correct in assuming that its "game" is to maintain life and the process of evolution for as long as they can be sustained, Man seems to be the most actively evolving living organism, and Nature's interest in him might be thought to be equivalent to his own. If Man fails to judge and act wisely in maintaining his life and the process of evolution, Nature can be expected to take an "active hand" in correcting his "errors." Accordingly, Man must try to know as much as possible about Nature's ways of "error-correcting," through mechanisms of "regulation and control," both for augmenting health and reducing disease, if he is to develop a niche in which he can also experience the greatest number of healthy, constructive, creative individuals. This implies a need to determine how to deal best with the problem posed by Nature's tendency to eliminate the unfit, or those who do not fit well, which differs from Man's tendency to try to preserve human life regardless of fitness.

It is unrealistic to believe that some utopian human state

could exist free from the operation of the laws of Nature. That Man can operate, collectively or individually, according to rules that defy, or are counter to, the laws of Nature is equally unreal. Similarly, Man's attempt to defy or oppose his BEING leads only to the kind of distress from which there is absolutely no escape, save an illusory one, that may be temporarily provided by diversion, through devotion or addiction to not altogether satisfying purposes *in* life, of the energy that is intended, in part, for fulfilling the purposes *of* life. Such escape is unnecessary if the purposes *of* life and the purposes chosen *in* one's life match the desires of the BEING. Since Man's BEING "desires" not only to fulfill the species' purpose of survival, and Nature's purposes in evolution, but to satisfy the individual, then Man's chosen purposes *in* life must in some way relate to each if the individual's BEING is to be fulfilled.

The contrasts coming into evidence in the transition from Epoch A to Epoch B show that there must exist in the germ plasm of Man, and hence in the human BEING, broadly speaking, desires to satisfy Nature, the species, and the individual's BEING, as well as a need to react aggressively against forces judged to be of opposite value. If so, it is of great practical as well as theoretical interest to understand the different tendencies now emerging as Man demonstrates his fitness for survival as a species comprised of diverse individuals and of groups. This requires a new set of human attributes different from those selected in the early history of Man. If Man were wise, he would try to understand and cooperate with the inevitability of these changes to which he can actively contribute as a fulfilling purpose *in* life as well as *of* life.

It is likely that the cost in human life of such changes will be considerable. The cost can be reduced, however, if Man will act with, not counter to, Nature. Hence he must understand Nature, so that he may cooperate with it to his advantage. The net effect might be not only a considerable reduction in conflict but an augmentation in productive and constructive work, as well as in *purpose* essential for a healthy, fulfilling human existence. This requires the kind of discipline seen in Nature, except at moments when life is near its end due to disease or age. Such discipline has to be educed and encouraged; the existing potential for it is realized only if challenged. This implies a need for the development of an EGO structure, for education and for training appropriate to fulfilling the potential of the BEING and its disciplined and restrained expression.

Man must learn to discriminate between the qualities of things if he is to distinguish the pathological from the healthy and if he is to improve the quality of his own life and of the lives of those to come. He must recognize the existence, among his numbers, of the destructive. Eventually, too, he must understand the causes, cures, and means for prevention of the physical or mental disturbances of human beings who, if impaired, can exert a great force for destruction.

Having set forth these views about health and disease, we now have to elaborate on what may be referred to as the EGO system in relation to the BEING system, and on relationships generally in the human realm, as these are revealed in the epochal changes through which Man is going.

XI

MAN,
HIS OWN VICTIM

THE NEED FOR a basic harmony between the BEING and the EGO also applies within each of the metabiological dualisms, including the attitudes and concepts arising from them. Similar dualisms operate in all transactions in Nature where the "seeking" of advantage is part of the evolutionary process. This is true in human relationships generally and is especially striking politically and economically. For this reason, Man must be aware of the dialectics in the evolutionary process, and of the alternative ways for resolving conflicts between antagonistic pairs if he himself is to avoid becoming a victim of his own creative and intellectual achievements.

The results of the evolutionary process show evidence of the selection of both destructive and constructive tendencies. This is seen in the pattern of increasingly complex systems, arising through the coalescence of molecules, cells, individuals, and groups, which seemingly possess mutually destructive elements or functions, yet are "chosen" in the selection process. Since that which persists in "competition" for survival appears to lead to greater evolutionary advantage, the process must, on balance, be more positive than negative. Perhaps, then, the word "preference," rather than "competition," more accurately describes the basis for Nature's "decision" to select.

This process is seen in the functioning of the immunological system, which serves to protect the "integrity" of the individual by acting destructively against "foreign" and potentially destructive organisms. In the course of time this system evolved to destroy what it "perceives" as foreign. Occasionally, however, one's own tissue, or self-tissue, is attacked, causing an autoimmune disease. Such an effect is autodestructive. However, the same process is autoprotective when activated against cancer cells, which are self-cells that have, in the course of cancerous transformation, become both malignant and "foreign." This system must be carefully regulated and controlled since its indiscriminate activity could be harmful to the organism whose integrity it evolved to protect. However, if neutralized *excessively* it could fail to carry out its protective function. For evolution to continue, its functional pattern must be predominantly protective and constructive, and only "usefully" destructive. Since psychological and sociological behavior resembles the way in which the immunological system operates, this suggests that Man is confronted by similar patterns within which choices must be made.

In general this implies a dualistic, relativistic, and dynamic attitude in which value judgments are expressed in developmental and evolutionary terms rather than in absolute and static terms; in the latter, fixed preconceptions, once laid down, serve as the basis for judgment even though these may be anti-evolutionary. Absolutists are extremists who see life exclusively from their own narrow, rigid viewpoint. They may play either revolutionary or conservative roles and yet be destroyed by their own inability to participate in the evolutionary process. Revolution and evolution are not synonymous. The former is part of the latter in the oscillations that characterize the process of selection both in biologic and metabiologic evolution.

Judgment as to what might be "wise" biologically or metabiologically is related to survival both of the species and of the individual. That which is of biological value has been judged by Nature through its processes of natural selection. That which will prove to be of metabiological value as well as biological will, in due course, be decided not only by Man but by Nature. Hence it behooves Man to become as wise as Nature—i.e., to use a value system corresponding to that of Nature—if he wishes to avoid errors in judgment for which he will have to pay the price of suffering which, if not corrected, will be a stage on the way to self-elimination or extinction. A characteristic of wisdom in Nature is the existence of alternative pathways and of more than one option, as evidenced, for example, in the coronary circulation in the heart, in the circle of Willis in the arterial system of the brain, in the multiple possibilities for immunologic defense against lethal agents, and in the variety of solutions possible for the psychologically and sociologically nonrigid and nonabsolute person who approaches life as a dynamic process.

It would follow that the BEING and EGO attributes of Man which are *pro-* rather than *anti*-evolution would be favored by Nature and would be signaled by subjective feelings of satisfaction and fulfillment. Or, stated another way, a feeling of satisfaction and fulfillment would be expected to be associated with participation in the process of evolution; feelings of frustration and anxiety are associated with not being so involved, or in not so acting when the opportunity exists.

An example of the need for exercise and use of potential for full functional development of biological structures is seen in the postnatal development of the visual system, in which permanent impairment results if the light-sensitive system is not exercised early in life. The same is true of the immunologic system and of the processes involved in language acquisition. In metabiological terms, the feeling of fulfillment is associated with extensions beyond the strictly biological, as in the feeling of fulfillment and satisfaction in raising children, in the work we do creatively or constructively, in contributing to the processes of growth, development, and evolution. If the energy available to be used in these ways is not so engaged, it could well be directed into nonfulfilling, uselessly destructive activities, which may also be satisfying in the sense of providing release from feelings of frustration and anxiety if not released constructively. Therefore it is necessary for Man generally to acquire what some *innately* possess, i.e., the wisdom to know the difference between the constructive and the uselessly destructive and to be able to act accordingly. We refer to awareness of the consequences of choices, and of alternatives leading either to continued existence in the process of being and becoming, or to destruction and nonexistence.

Wisdom has at least persisted in the course of human history. Now we are saying that if the quality of human life is to improve, the processes of selection, both natural and human, will have to choose the wisest for positions of influence and of power. Eventually, the struggle in the human domain will be between the wise and the nonwise. This implies that those who lead others in ways that are anti-evolutionary, or that are counter to the natural process of becoming of the BEING, will either be replaced by others possessing wisdom akin to that of Nature, to guide men toward survival with greater satisfaction and fulfillment, or lead Man to disaster.

If we think of wisdom as the art of the disciplined use of imagination in respect to alternatives, exercised at the right time and in the right measure, it is apparent that judgment is required as to what is "right," in time and in measure. This may well depend upon an *innate* art, for which, in part at least, a science can be developed to serve as a guide, and a basis for judgment, for those who do not possess the imagination, or the art, within themselves. They could, thereby, be helped to function and to relate in ways that are constructive, rather than uselessly destructive, to their own BEINGS and to others, and in this way experience a greater measure of satisfaction and fulfillment in life, rather than more anxiety and frustration.

Men and women of wisdom have survived as part of a long and continuous process. If the wisest prevail, the outcome will be interesting to witness. If the nonwise prevail, the effects will be catastrophic and will take the form of what has been imagined by writers of fiction who have projected into the future a behavior based upon unwisdom.

The sense of being and becoming, of which the wise are more conscious than others, is part of an awareness of the process of life in evolution. The nature of the questions about which Man must make judgments and choices is reflected in the words listed in Table I. Two sets of attitudes are implied by the two columns, both of which must be reconciled in a balanced way relative to each other, inasmuch as one without the other is meaningless. These lists can be extended by the addition of many other examples of similar pairs of opposed complementaries, revealing the detailed complexity of this simple pattern of dualisms. In this way constancy with diversity is replicated as part of the order in Nature and also in the human realm.

TABLE I

Being	—	Becoming
Absolute	—	Relative
Parts	—	Whole
Extremes	—	Balance
Quantity	—	Quality
Present	—	Future

In the list of words compared in Table II, and the meanings implied by them, we see the basis for disagreement and disorder in the metabiological realm, and the need for their reconciliation by an *and* rather than an *or* attitude. It is no more reasonable to consider the genetic *or* somatic systems

TABLE II

Biological	—	Somatic	—	Genetic
		Individual	—	Species
Metabiological	—	EGO	—	BEING
		Intellect	—	Intuition
		Reason	—	Feeling
		Objective	—	Subjective
		Morality	—	Reality
		Differences	—	Differentiation
		Competition	—	Cooperation
		Power	—	Influence
		Win-Lose	—	Double-Win

separately, or in terms of dominance, since *both* the genetic *and* somatic systems are essential elements of a living organism—in a state of being and becoming. The development of the BEING and EGO systems of Man also depend upon inclusion and affirmation so as to favor growth, development, and evolution biologically and metabiologically, while denying and excluding anything harmful. In so doing Nature exercises what might be called wisdom. Since "errors," in a sense, occur in the course of this process, ways for error-correcting also exist in surviving living systems. Since one form of error-correcting operates through a process of elimination by natural selection of those "unfit" for survival and evolution, those forms which *do* persist must, by definition, possess hereditarily transmissible means for preventing their own elimination. This applies primarily to attributes which contribute to survival through the reproductive period regardless of the course of subsequent events. Thus biological forms which have survived perpetuate mechanisms for preventing and correcting "errors" that affect survival and that occur prior to or as part of the stage of procreation. One way devised in Nature for producing such effects is exemplified by the sigmoid curve of population growth, which reveals that survival depends upon the development of means for the adjustment of the behavior of individuals appropriate to protection from autodestruction.

It is for this reason, too, that changes in values are needed, and will inevitably take place in the metabiological realm, if biological survival is to be accompanied by improvement in the quality of life, including increasing satisfaction and fulfillment for the individual. For this it will be necessary to develop attitudes that are appropriate from the species as well as the individual point of view, and to augment means of cooperation, and eventually coalescence, toward the formation of the organism of mankind in which "double-win" and "win-lose" resolutions are employed appropriately. Those "who fit best" as well as "the fittest" will be chosen for survival in a differentiated organization in which the value of individual and group differences are retained so long as they are not autodestructive or anti-evolutionary. Judgments in this regard, to bring Man's agenda and Nature's agenda into closer harmony, clearly require wisdom. To adjust Man's game to conform to that of Nature, by the application of Nature's principles, Man's intuitional and intellectual attributes will be needed. A set of principles of metabiology could be of value to guide the development of the BEING and EGO of Man and for applying science and art in dealing with problems related both to life and to death. In so doing it will be necessary to distinguish between, yet relate, knowledge and wisdom, reality and morality, materialism and idealism, reason and feeling, objective and subjective, verbal and nonverbal, absolute and relative.

As everything in evolution is antagonistic and protagonistic, Man is similarly constructed. He is now engaged in a struggle between two sets of forces which can either act separately or together and be either mutually opposing or mutually reinforcing. The ideas conveyed by the paired words in Tables I and II imply the need on the part of Man to be conscious of their meaning in his life in order for him to develop awareness and understanding of the processes working upon him and within him. These lists contain sets of opposed complementaries which have to be reconciled by an *and* rather than *or* attitude, and by actions and a way of life consistent therewith.

From the foregoing examples it becomes possible to see the difference between the tendencies that have prevailed in Epoch A and trends developing in Epoch B; those which prevailed in the past reflected the prevalence of the *or* rather than the *and* attitude, with the dominance of individual and EGO attitudes. Now, an *and* attitude together with a species and BEING orientation are coming more and more into evidence, in part by necessity and in part as a matter of choice by those who sense what is needed to contribute to the survival of the species. Table III indicates the changing

TABLE III

Epoch A	Epoch B
Anti-Death	Pro-Life
Anti-Disease	Pro-Health
Death Control	Birth Control
Self-Repression	Self-Expression
External Restraint	Self-Restraint

trends and values, with reconciliation of the complementary patterns that are now converging and intertwining in a mutually reinforcing way.

Man does have a choice, i.e., either to cooperate with the process or not. These are his alternatives. It is a matter neither for pessimism nor for optimism. It does, however, relate to his individual and collective state of "development" and of "health," and of the capacity for continuation, or not, in the evolutionary stream. As in Nature generally, there will be men who will endure and those who will not—groups and types that will survive and those that will not. Nature has its way of choosing. It may comfort some, and distress others, to know where they stand in the scheme of things, when the human and cosmic games are exposed and counterposed. It does not take too much wisdom to predict who will be favored, since Nature and *not men* will, in effect, have the last word. It is why we speak of the need for *awareness*, and for the *and* attitude, and for *wisdom*, on the part of those who might wish to persist if only for the pleasure derived from the process of so doing.

When one sees the way in which Man has been developing and considers the role played in his cultural evolution by desire, it becomes obvious that its fulfillment could provide him with a great deal of pleasure and satisfaction if he were to have greater understanding of those forces and would conduct his life with greater harmony. He would contribute by example to the development of the lives of others so as to lead toward more cooperation, coalescence, and cohesion. For this to be effective, we must understand the preconditions required. In itself, it is a gigantic challenge, one for which no individual can possibly be fully or adequately equipped. A state of general awareness is required to release the power of association, while removing, or neutralizing, the forces of dissociation. Man needs new goals toward which to move consciously and with trust. The extent to which this trust can prevail, along with a guarded awareness of its absence or its opposite, will determine the possibility and the extent of the outcome of his evolution.

Again, it is for these reasons that we speak of the survival of the wisest. This, now, takes on the aspect of reality and not prophecy, the validity of which time alone can reveal. However, if Man is conscious of the processes working on him and within him, he may be able to exercise whatever measure of free will he possesses, within the possibilities of the prevailing circumstances, to change and bring his talents to bear, in influencing the direction of human evolution. His success or failure will depend equally upon errors of omission as upon errors of commission. For this reason, consciousness as well as wisdom is required for success in such an endeavor.

The correspondence between biological wisdom and meta-biological wisdom should have become clear from the examples cited. Thus the meaning of the words "wisdom of Nature" and the "wisdom of Man" have been brought together through the meaning of each for survival of the species and for the quality of human life in terms of individual satisfaction and fulfillment. Toward fulfilling this dual purpose some men have begun to move consciously as they have become aware of their responsibility to express their own BEING in Nature.

XII

THE PHILOSOPHY
OF "AND"

In an attempt to state concisely the difference between the recent past in human history and what is imagined
for the future, Figure 18 was drawn to suggest that the difference is essentially between a philosophy, or attitude
described by the word *"or,"* for the past, and the word *"and,"*
for the future. This suggests that in the future it will be necessary for Man to relate to Nature complementarily (*and*)
rather than exclusively (*either/or*). For example, when Man
began to see himself as separate from Nature and tried to conquer, subdue, or outdo it by the use of his intellectual powers,
and by the knowledge and skills he developed, he brought
about an imbalance between his BEING and his EGO. A change
occurred from a life in which he lived close to, and part of,
Nature, to one in which he became increasingly separated
from it and artificially related to it, through his dependence
upon the many support systems developed for living this way.

To abandon scientific and technologic help for human life
would be to court disaster on a scale hitherto unknown in
the history of Man; and to fail to modulate the extent to

79

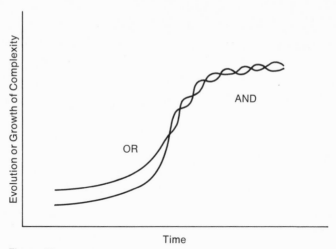

Figure 18

which Man has become separated from his own BEING would be equally disastrous. Hence the consciousness of these effects of human evolutionary development have given birth to movements aimed at correcting these relative excesses and insufficiencies. These movements are future-oriented. They aim to obliterate the separateness of the past, and have the characteristics of an *and* rather than an *or* philosophy—an "additive" philosophy rather than an "alternative" one. They want to relate to other, similar movements and to keep away from those that are sensed to be otherwise. The "enemy" is now beginning to be seen not as those who may be part of the other main stem, or part of another branch (see Figure 14, page 26) but rather as those who are "pathologically divisive" or "destructive" of the unification and coalescence of healthy, contributing, constructive elements of a greater complexity, necessary to solve the problems of existence in Man's relationship to his own BEING to others and to the universe.

The foregoing is not meant to be an exercise in abstraction, but rather a way of seeing the problems of Man with as much perspective as is now possible. A great convergence is occurring among those with similar realizations or appreciation of reality, and there is great readiness among many to arrive at a common understanding to reduce and eventually to eliminate the waste and destruction that Man has come to support. Waste and destruction have become a way of life for many who are reluctant to relinquish or change this basis for their existence and livelihood even though it may be at the expense of others, of the resources of the species, of the ecosystem, and of the planet. It will be necessary, in time, to distinguish the healthy from the pathological in these respects and to establish an ethic that can be conveyed in a metaphor useful for helping Man to behave in a pro-life, pro-evolutionary fashion, rather than in an anti-life and anti-evolutionary one. That which was, and is, anti-life, expressed in genocide, is as much an evolutionary phenomenon as what is here thought of as a new ethic and a new morality on the basis of which Man's future survival as a species and as an individual is dependent.

Thus we must look into the past and assimilate the lessons of biological and human history, not for repetition but rather to learn how to avoid errors in order to see what can be improved, and what must now be done, to be able to live healthfully, and to develop and evolve, producing, in part, the circumstances that will define the future. This will require a deep consciousness of others as well as ourselves, enabling us to understand what others mean, and to relate to them on the basis not of what they say but of what they mean, in terms of evolution of the individual and of the species. In this way we shall develop the necessary new educational systems and techniques for accomplishing such purposes, if we are convinced that they are among the important contributions needed now and in the future.

The sense of urgency is strong, especially among the young. They feel committed, they compare the consciousness they have of their BEINGS with that of others in relation to the needs of their time, as they try to correct the errors of the past. They are but a part of a larger group whose awareness has increased through their experiences in life, and who see and interpret the changes that have been occurring in the human realm in essentially the same way. A new body of conscious individuals exists, expressing its desire for a better life for Man as a species and as individuals, eager to devote themselves to this end. Such groups, when they are able to coalesce through an understanding of their relatedness to one another and to the natural processes involved in "Nature's game" of survival and evolution, will find strength and courage in sensing themselves as a part of the Cosmos and as being involved in a game that is in accord with Nature and not anti-natural. These groups will initiate movements which, in turn, will be manifest in their effects not only upon the species and the planet but upon individual lives. Their benefit is likely to be expressed in a greater frequency, or proportion, of individuals finding increasing satisfaction and fulfillment in life.

These factors, among others, would be a valid reason for expanding consciousness of reality and for adjusting "Man's game" to "Nature's game." In terms of human evolution, the consequences would soon be seen. It would have the short-term effect of contributing toward increasing pleasure and satisfaction in life and diminishing displeasure and dissatisfaction, which, in the past, were generally thought to be a necessary prerequisite for a better life in some hereafter. Such endeavors may be the way of wisdom.

It will be necessary to develop, from birth, an educational system designed to produce these effects consciously, deliberately, and as effectively as possible.

It is important to recognize the necessity for developing the imagination and curiosity in the BEING whence comes the integrative capacity of the mind, which continues to function even in sleep, perhaps especially then. In wakefulness, associations are more easily made by minds which are allowed to be as agile as possible and not frightened into submission by fixed ways of thinking or filled or blocked by taboos which negate what is sensed by the BEING. Whether evidence does or does not yet exist as to the effect of development in the imaginative functions (of the BEING) upon the cognitive development (of the EGO), it can be postulated that the effect will be strongly positive if *both* are trained with equal vigor and not, as often happens, that one is favored over the other in an unbalanced way. This could have a salutary effect and encourage the emergence of more balanced persons who are healthier metabiologically and who might become wise not only in the course of surviving the vicissitudes of the past but in the course of life as a positive experience. If a new morality is to emerge, and if the wisest are to endure and their descendants to survive, it will be because they will have found a way to learn and to teach their wisdom in a world they have inherited and which seems to be ripe for this kind of metamorphosis. The new world we visualize will be one in which the fittest to persist will also be those who fit best in a pattern designed to fit the purpose of Nature for the survival of the species and the satisfaction of constructive individuals.

If we wish to reduce the number of those who are purposelessly destructive without, at the same time, adversely affecting the evolutionary process, we will have to distinguish between useful and nonuseful destructive behavior. For example, in contests in which the fittest were tested for survival in Nature, attributes were selected that served to increase the probability of success and, therefore, traits were selected which served for protection against destruction in win-lose contests. War is a product of metabiological evolution, with the development of the BEING and EGO, and of the imaginative and intellectual faculties, without an as yet sufficiently sophisticated system for conflict resolution beyond that of intraspecies killing. While this sort of conflict resolution may have served, in the past, for selection in evolution, it may also have resulted in reducing the number of those who opposed war and might have developed other solutions to conflicts but who did not possess what was necessary to escape destruction. Hence we who exist today are the descendants of the survivors of such a process, hence the destructive and counterdestructive activity. At the present point in human evolution, however, such destructiveness seems useless, wasteful, and too costly, even though great progress in solving problems useful in peacetime has been made during wartime. The question logically arises whether substitute means for coping with these residues of evolutionarily valuable destructiveness and defensive counterdestructivity can be developed without eliminating that useful destruction which is part of the evolutionary process.

The point made here is the necessity of discovering ways of reducing and preventing pathology in the metabiological system, just as we struggle to reduce disease in the biological systems of Man. It is to be expected that few are innately or by experience equipped to take the initiative in providing others with example and leadership toward the necessary goal. Such a goal is many leagues beyond those individually envisioned by most leaders. However, it is not beyond the vision of those who have developed consciousness of the problems and the needs required for the journey, which will take years and will demand great wisdom. The resources and the plans required have to be worked out carefully. It is not something to be accomplished quickly, nor to be delayed either. Enough individuals and institutions possess similar insights and have only to be encouraged to follow the dictates of their own BEINGS—and to find one another. They will discover the resources within themselves and in each other to overcome the resistance, difficulties, and skepticism, as well as cynicism, of those who are either blind or who disbelieve that the aggressive tendencies in Man can be *constructively* "exploited" to change the complexion of human life.

Imagining that life continues in some form after death is a harmless faith so long as it does not promise rewards for otherwise avoidable deprivations in life on earth. Ethical or moral systems based upon promises for which proof of reward cannot be established permit the exploitation of Man's capacity to believe to the point where he is rendered ineffective, victimized in the development and expression of his BEING. Thus arises the obligation for truth in dealing with Man, even though metaphor and analogy are necessary to communicate the nature of reality to the young, especially, in a form closest to that revealed by scientific methods. This does not preclude other ways of perceiving, comprehending, and communicating reality, as through the methods of the artist. In fact, it is necessary that both methods be employed.

The artist draws largely upon that part of the mind that functions beneath consciousness, even in sleep, while the scientist by and large, but not exclusively, uses that part of the mind that functions in consciousness. The part of the mind that functions beneath consciousness also operates during consciousness; but it is necessary to learn how to draw more upon it and employ it for solving the problems of life, of survival, and of evolution. Wisdom arises from both parts of the mind. The system of recognition and application of the part of the mind which rationalizes then brings to realization the insights derived from the source of "native wisdom" for which "objective proof" may not yet exist.

It would follow from the foregoing that there is a need to find ways of increasing human awareness and consciousness of the processes that occur in the biological and metabiological systems of the growing individual and to become mindful of the effect of these and of Man's behavior upon his evolution. To the extent that Man is neither aware nor conscious of the meaning of his choices, and therefore neither aware nor conscious of the forces operating in him and upon him, he is not contributing as fully as he might in the exercise of judgment to fulfill his potential, or in deriving the greatest amount of satisfaction in life and contributing to his own life and to those of others.

As indicated in the preceding chapters, the diagrams presented in this book are intended to help us visualize what may be "known" to Man's BEING and expressed in different ways. The object is to offer a way of looking at problems and conceivable solutions in the human or metabiological realm in both intellectually *and* intuitively satisfying ways. A large part of the difficulty of the human condition is due to a dissociation between intellect and intuition, a division that has been greatly exaggerated as knowledge has increased and earlier beliefs have been brought into question.

A new and consciously attained system of balanced use of the brain's two aspects—the imaginative and the cognitive—is vitally necessary today. Such balance will be of great value to Man now and in the future, especially if the different value systems that are in conflict arise from the two different systems referred to as the BEING and the EGO, each dependent upon the other. All the way from the early stage of supreme narcissism, at birth, to the later stages of wisdom, both are required for Man to function as a BEING in a state of becoming. Even though this is an idealization, it provides a way to guide human expectations and achievements. If Man cannot attain the totality of the ideal, at least there remains a part, of which we are conscious, that is still possible. If Man is at the end of what is referred to as Epoch A, and at the beginning of Epoch B, and if we appreciate how long it has taken him to reach this stage, *we can then appreciate the nature of the problem with which he is now confronted.*

However, there is a very important difference now, as compared to the circumstances that existed heretofore. It is reflected not only in the increasing numbers who come upon the scene in a single generation, as compared to earlier generations, but in the greater proportion of individuals exposed to education and to the mass media, which increase, by orders of magnitude, the degree of consciousness of truth in the individual, as well as the opportunity for being misled by falsehood. Thus the situation with which Man is confronted is clearly different, as can be seen by the diagrams, from that which existed heretofore. The difference in the extent to which educational opportunities have increased in the United States in recent years is shown by the data in

Years of School Completed for Population
Cohort Age 35 to 39 by Decades, 1900 to 1980

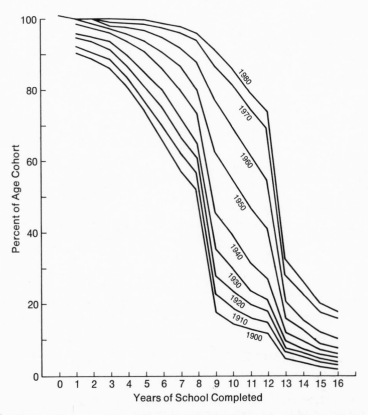

Figure 19. Source: Byrnes, James C., "The Quantity of Formal Instruction in the United States," Educational Policy Research Center, Syracuse University Research Corporation, February, 1970.

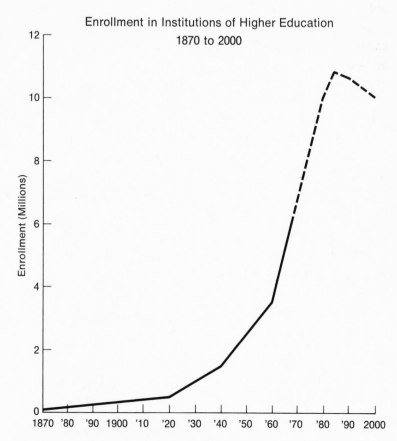

Enrollment in Institutions of Higher Education
1870 to 2000

Figure 20. Source: *Quality and Equality: New Levels of Federal Respon-sibility for Higher Education,* Copyright © 1968, Carnegie Foundation for the Advancement of Teaching. Used with permission of McGraw-Hill Book Company.

Figures 19 and 20. If we add to this the advent of television and an increased access to journalistic material which may not adhere to the tradition of truth as much as we would hope, it becomes possible to see the potentially explosive nature of this particular period of human history. The imbalance in the world among regions and nations with respect to educational opportunities and access to mass media creates a potentially more dangerous situation even than the economic disparities, when awareness and consciousness extend into parts of the world which have been disadvantaged in this regard. We are moving toward a state in the course of human evolution that can be considered revolutionary, as implied in the diagram (Figure 17, page 59) depicting the alternative trajectories, which depend mainly on whether or not Man is successful in developing an operating attitude as suggested in the diagram (Figure 18, page 80) concerning an *and* ("additive") rather than an *or* ("alternative") relationship. The following chapters will attempt to reveal the complexity and difficulty of the problem in the present state of the world and to show the need for integrative thinking in respect to the BEING and the EGO.

XIII

EMERGENCE
OF BEING FROM
EGO DOMINATION

PERHAPS the most important change now occurring in Man's consciousness is knowledge of threats to the survival of the human species by what might be thought of as "errors" of commission and of omission. More individuals are becoming aware of their responsibility for the welfare of their species and life on the planet, not merely of their responsibility for their own person and those immediately related to them. There is increased understanding that the harmful effects of group or national selfishness must be reduced and eliminated while at the same time the advantages of cultural distinctiveness and individual uniqueness are preserved.

There is on the part of some an acceptance of the fact that what is advantageous at one time or from one point of view can be, and often is, disadvantageous at another time or from another point of view. Wisdom is composed of this kind of consciousness. It is also important to develop increased awareness of the meaning of each advantage, in terms of both survival and evolution, if we want to be able to deal wisely, and in a balanced way, with other people's inclina-

tions and tendencies as well as our own. We must see the
point of view of alternative possibilities if we are to contribute wisely to the solution of our own metabiological problems
and to deal with those of others as they impinge upon us,
near or far.

Such increased awareness can only come with the development of sufficient perspective—from trying to see the whole
of the process of which we are a part—so that we might then
be able to cope better with feelings of threat, to which
we often respond unconsciously, reacting in a way that moves
away from rather than toward proper resolution, or solution.

We must provide a broader perspective of the process of
evolution in the metabiological realm. We shall speak of the
existence of what seem to be "pseudo species" within the
human species, and of the opposite trend toward the development of an organism of mankind in which such differences
and conflicts as still exist might be of a constructive sort,
reducing purposeless destruction. Whether or not the latter
will be realized is the main issue of our time. Nevertheless,
consciousness of this possibility is a prerequisite for Man's
ability to cope with foresight and deliberation rather than
impulsively and rashly.

It will be necessary for all of us to see ourselves and others
from the same point of view. This opportunity is afforded by
the diagrams which have been proposed and on which we
may find ourselves, in relation to time and to Mankind in the
evolutionary process. We may also see the effect of time and
circumstances upon us and become conscious of the alternatives from which we may choose, and the consequences
thereof. We also see the effect of choice by others and the
necessity for working in concert with them if we are to realize
mutually desired objectives. At least, we will be able to rec-

ognize our objective, as revealed by these illustrations, and be conscious of those desired generally and how they all may be reconciled. We can see whereby each may gain something toward their end, and how to arrest the clearly destructive and pathological, who must be judged in evolutionary terms.

It would seem from the diagrams that there exists in biological entities a permanent instability tending, or reaching, toward stability. This operates apparently through an increasing diversity and a concomitant tendency to uniformity, through selection for stability and capacity for diversity, variety, and relationship. These seemingly mutually exclusive tendencies are part of the same process, which would cease if any succeeded in eliminating one of the others. Therefore, in order to remain part of such a process, it is necessary to be able to function in it and to develop and evolve so as to contribute to it. It is even necessary to be, at one and the same time, objective as well as subjective, to develop the ability to function while guarding, guiding, and disciplining the growth and expression of one's own BEING as a necessary part of this interacting process.

In such a situation one is like the product of the interaction of a canvas and an artist. The artist may be thought of as the BEING and EGO of the person, the canvas and the materials as the constituents of circumstances referred to as reality, and the painting as the resultant effect of this interaction. A successful painting requires time and peace to allow both BEING and EGO to react and to create out of reality an expression of the very essence of life which will subsequently provide a model able to help other men to function in the same way.

The role of the individual in suppressing "destroyers" of life and in dealing with noncontributors cannot be minimized, since in Man, and among men, the actuality and the potentiality exist to destroy as well as to inhibit the growth, development, and evolution of the BEING.

Let us look at the diagram in Figure 16 (page 58) from this point of view. If the foregoing hypothesis is correct, we might interpret the convergence of lines at the point of inflection in the growth curves as the emergence of the BEING from domination and suppression by the EGO, in larger and larger numbers of individuals, and in the increased recognition of the need to develop an EGO-BEING relationship such as is suggested by the intertwining lines, implying a relationship in which the EGO serves the BEING, facilitating its development and expression, and in which the EGO is developed so as not to be dominated by other EGOS. Individuals constructed in this way would fit well into hierarchies of purpose, where domination, subservience, and exclusivity do not operate, but which facilitate and help the process of survival and evolution of the individual and the species in a way that enhances the fulfillment of the individual. This is what the diagrams suggest as the ideal toward which the separated lines are trending. They also suggest that other forces are operating and that this ideal is therefore not universally attainable, but constitutes a state toward which all may strive within the limits of their capacity and of opportunity. They thus reveal not only the nature of the process but the nature of the problems associated therewith, and the tendencies to be overcome as well as the trends to be reinforced if Man, individually and collectively, is to be able to cope with the difficulties involved in expressing the essence of life.

Thus, if one of the most important driving forces in Man is the emergence of the BEING, then the figures indicate the nature of the difficulties to be overcome. They also indicate the individual and the collective nature of the way in which individuals are relating, and will very likely be more and more inclined to interact as time goes on. They also suggest the endless nature of the operation and the extent to which each human life has to be active if the individual is to become a satisfied and fulfilled participant. They reveal the importance of relationship and the consequences of separation and of alienation from those with whom it is necessary to be associated for one's own satisfaction and the fullest development and expression of one's own BEING. They show the nature and importance of the connection not only between EGO and BEING but between the EGO-BEING systems of different individuals and the consequences of failures in such relationships.

The diagrams do not tell how to develop the BEING and EGO systems nor how to develop relationships. They do, however, indicate that we need to be more than simply cognizant of Nature's pattern, of which we are a part, and of our metabiological patterns. We need to learn to use our consciousness, to facilitate the healthy development of the young, enabling them to continue their own harmonious development. This knowledge could then be employed to help the expression, through the EGO, of the unconscious patterns and forces of the BEING toward constructive, creative purposes in a hierarchy based upon native talents and abilities and the disciplined capacity to perform and grow to the satisfaction and fulfillment of the individual. We must, in short, develop the kind of wisdom that would keep the BEING and EGO systems in a balanced relationship within the boundaries of excess and insufficiency. What is required is the kind of constant, disciplined management of these relationships and forces that would give rise to a performance in life corresponding to that of a well-trained athlete, dancer, painter, writer, scientist, engineer, or any of the other man-practiced arts.

The biological counterparts of the metabiological processes required for wisdom are essentially the product of experience —the result of mutation and selection, or, one might say, trial and error or trial and success. In a sense, new patterns or ideas arising in the BEING and acted out by EGO-constructed means would correspond to the new mutations arising in the genes and expressed somatically and functionally.

The diagrams show the necessity of a relation between the BEING and EGO systems which will serve the BEING. If not frustrated, the individual is likely to develop species- as well as self-interest and concern and therefore become a more open person relating with other like beings. They also suggest that the intelligence and the intuition need to be associated in the same way, so that the intellect can play with intuitive signals and messages, and objectivity can take subjectivity into account as a source of data to be weighed in formulating judgments. The greater need, in the future, is for the exercise of "domination" of the EGO systems *by the* BEING rather than domination *by others.* Another way of saying this is: not the domination *of or by others* but rather the *disciplined expression of one's own* BEING *in a reciprocal relationship between* BEING *and* EGO. The tendency of the past, to seek the *domination of others,* or the *domination of many by a few,* will not be tolerated for very long, now that the process of evolution of the metabiological systems of Man has reached its present point, with the degree of actual emergence of the BEING already evident within many different cultures and in many areas of the world.

Finally, the diagrams suggest that this emergence has occurred, in part, because of the excesses that economic, political, religious, technological, and other sociological forces have engendered in exercising restraints as well as repression of the BEING. The social effects of such excesses, together with increased liberation in the way of greater knowledge on the part of more people plus increased economic advantages, have tended to discredit or challenge previously existent authority. Such EGO-mediated restraints have weakened, and the forces of the BEING have been released. Concomitantly, the necessary discipline of the BEING has not as yet developed, in all instances, for as meaningful self-expression as is possible. Hence, it could be expected that unrestrained, unbridled, and undisciplined expression of the BEING, without an adequately developed EGO, would lead to excesses in the opposite extreme to what had been observed under circumstances of punitive self-repression by "hypertrophied" EGO systems "externally" oriented to serve the demands of religious, cultural, social, and political forces whose object was to control the creativity of the individual BEING. By the same token, a human life dominated by a BEING which was malfunctioning, unbalanced by objective considerations such as the unyielding reality of Nature or the particular circumstances of existence, would result in another kind of eccentricity. The operation of, and respect for, intuitive considerations only, without development and use of the intellect, would give rise to similar effects.

While there has until now been a dominance of external controls over the BEING, mediated through EGO-controlling factors—as in puritanism, for example, or in enforced social and political conformity—and while the dominance of "objectivity" and of "intellectuality" has prevailed so far, in the Western world, the tendency toward the other extreme would lead to equally undesirable consequences. Thus this tendency toward overemphasis of one or the other of two complementary elements of the pairs in a dualism, leading to *either/or* judgments and behavior, needs to be balanced by *and* type considerations. These require appropriate and adequate development of the BEING *and* EGO systems of the individual *and* of the society.

There is a close similarity between personal and social philosophy in a balanced relationship of individuals with healthy BEING-EGO systems. Conversely, where the personal needs of the BEING, especially of the most highly evolved and most highly developed individuals, are not satisfied, any social or political philosophy which is at variance with such needs will, in due course, be challenged. The society may be forced to yield, to allow individuals more freedom to live with their own BEINGS and with their fellow men in a system which protects the species' interest but does not thwart the interests of creative BEINGS. Thus both the protection of self-expression and species preservation and evolution must be guaranteed by any viable political, social, and economic system, inasmuch as the individual BEING is the inexorable source of the creative and evolutionary force.

The emergence of the human BEING has developed to a point at which it is not capable of relating to outmoded EGO systems and forces as suggested in the diagrams referring to the past. This is as important an event in the evolutionary process as any other survival-testing event of a new species in the course of evolution. Man will soon have proof of his capacity to persist in his own presence. It is certain that, until previously arising species demonstrated their capacity to react with feedback-controlled responses, they, too, went through the kind of test for survival that is now occurring in Man. While most humans who need to respond in this manner are not yet fully controlled in this way, signs appear that men exist who feel and react, intuitively and intellectually, more strongly than others to the demands of Nature for the exercise of such controls, through the adoption of value systems appropriate for the time in which they live, and in anticipation of the continuing need to adjust values, ethics, and morals to the circumstances of life, for survival, evolution, and human satisfaction. Thus in respect to evolution metabiological considerations must be taken into account with as great seriousness as ecological ones.

Having said this, it becomes necessary to understand those metabiological considerations that are important for continued improvement of the quality of life. The suppression of the development and expression of the BEING leads to its deterioration, followed by the disintegration and destruction of the individual as a fully functioning unit. Under such circumstances, mass disaster would be expected to ensue, out of which might arise a new variety of Man from a hardy core with the strength and capacity of their BEING to adapt to the changed circumstances. *Such individuals might prove to have possessed the "wisdom" to survive.*

XIV

TRANSITION
FROM EPOCH A
TO EPOCH B

It should now be clear that the BEING-EGO systems must function together in a balanced way just as the genetic-somatic systems must. This is as true of the intuitive-intellectual system, of the species and the individual, of the organism and its cells, as of the cells and their constituents. Each of these is an example of the relationship between the whole and the parts, between quality and quantity. The same relationship must be true of the future and the present, of becoming and being. It is also true of the relationship between the general and the particular, laws and rules, life and death, questions and answers, wisdom and knowledge. They are different complementary programs which involve Nature and Man. They now require the same kind of detailed examination and analysis under the heading of metabiology. From these analogies we might expect to gain ideas and knowledge for application to the practical problems of recognizing and developing the BEING and EGO systems in a way leading to the enhancement of balance in the person, in being, and in becoming, and hence to the enhancement of balance in the species. It seems that a thorough understanding of the BEING-EGO systems of the individual, and of the requirements for their expression, maturation, and function, might help us go a long way toward establishing the preconditions for peace among Mankind. Unless we place such emphasis upon the need to understand equilibrium in all aspects of the human organism, individually and collectively, including the BEING-EGO systems of the individual, we will always be predominantly preoccupied with the pathological, with reducing the negative rather than enhancing the positive. Until we see the sources of pathology as partly attributable to ignorance of what is required for maintaining health, we will continue to search for causes which can be eliminated or prevented, when, in fact, some of the pathology we seek to suppress is the result of our failure to do certain things that actively evoke and maintain a state of balance.

This discussion is germane to the problem which faces Man as we go through the transition from Epoch A to Epoch B. We are entering a time in which there will be greater consciousness of the *health of the individual for species survival*. There will be greater interest in the *quality* of the individual, rather than in quantity, *for guaranteeing the survival of the species*. From our diagrams it would seem logical that when sufficient numbers have been produced within the limits of the system, the energy involved in the process of growth will find better expression in directions that deal with quality, rather than with quantity alone. Hence we can recognize a change in attitude toward quantity and quality *in relation to people* as we go through the period of transition from the state of Man as described by Curve A to the one described by Curve B. Paradoxically, Man himself has, in the past, been more interested in the quality of the things he made (often at the expense of other men) as in his artifacts and great monuments of art. This has been true of craftsmen, artists, philosophers, and scientists generally. As Epoch A begins to come to an end, an emphasis on quantity at the sacrifice of quality has emerged which may well be partly responsible for the current revolt leading to the end of Epoch A. The beginning of Epoch B manifests changes in values aimed at the aesthetic satisfaction of more sensitive and articulate individuals, even though the masses may, for a variety of reasons, be insensitive to or ignorant of what is happening, although adversely affected themselves by the former value system. It is necessary therefore that each individual contribute, to the limit of the endowment and development of his BEING-EGO system, to the improvement of the metabiological conditions of Man and toward the reduction of the amount of pathology attributable to maldevelopment or malfunctioning of the metabiological processes in Man.

It will be necessary not only to develop the science and applied arts of metabiology but to educate and train all individuals in the practice of this science and art in everyday life. It will no longer be possible, in the world described by Curve B, to continue to educate in the manner of the world described by Curve A. There will, of course, be a need for education, in the sense of educing what is latent in the BEING in a state of becoming, and for teaching, in the sense of imparting knowledge to each person so he may develop the skills necessary for realizing the potential of his own BEING-EGO system. The individual will need knowledge in order for him to respond to the new and different circumstances of life as they develop around him, that he may contribute to the nurturing of a life satisfying to Man yet not at cross-purposes with Nature.

An educational system designed toward these goals will be quite different from one designed principally to provide training for economic independence. The latter is quite different from the teaching necessary to permit the individual to discover his BEING and to find a self-satisfying activity as well as economic stability. It should be clear, from this, to what extent malformed and malfunctioning individuals exist, especially in the so-called more advanced, industrialized societies, where the aims *in* life, to which an individual is devoted, are far removed from the purposes *of* life, for the fulfillment of which he was "designed" to satisfy. Very few indeed are those individuals today who find their niche in life in any one of the various occupations from which they can choose, and who are satisfied in them. On the contrary, many feel frustrated and are eager to revolt. Others suffer quietly, aware of the difficulties, but without the strength or the possibility of changing their lot in life. Still others are ignorant of the reasons for their suffering. Hence the quantity of active or latent unrest, of disguised distress as manifested in behavior patterns and in psychosomatic disorders, is considerable. While this situation is often attributed to society, or to other individuals, or to "errors" of the past, the fact is that it is in the nature of Man, in his metabiological development, that his difficulties lie. If he is to find a way out by his own devising, he must become conscious of the metabiological side of his nature in order to correct its deficiency states, as well as the excesses by which he tends to compensate for deficiencies in other areas. Just as we speak of *metabolic* diseases, we may well speak of *metabiologic* diseases, or of the nature and causes of Man's distress at the present time. He has been able to treat many of the infectious diseases and many of the nutritional and metabolic diseases (except those attributable to economic factors). Now, however, the most prominent kind of disorder in him appears to be in the metabiological realm.

It may be necessary to re-examine and develop another attitude toward the so-called *neuroses* from the point of view of cause and effect. It will help to determine to what extent effects become causes, when the difficulty lies in the metabiological realm and the disorder is due to maldevelopment or malfunctioning of the BEING and the EGO systems. In either case it is necessary to understand the nature of the disorder of the component parts of the BEING-EGO systems, whether "physiological" (in the sense of malfunctioning) or "anatomical" (in the sense of maldevelopment), and the nature of either, in terms of pathogenesis (i.e., origin of the dysfunction). In this way it will become possible to determine how to prevent, or to correct, either maldevelopment or malfunction and to understand what are the innate qualities in Man whose balanced development would prevent the metabiological disorders that must be endured or corrected later in life.

The attitude that Man is, by definition, born with "diseases," and that his life must consist, in part, in reducing the negative, is primarily a "disease-oriented attitude." The alternative attitude—that maldevelopment and malfunction of the metabiological system *can* lead to disease—assumes the existence, by and large, of a "natural" state of "health," which is subject to dysfunction as a result of postnatal influences. We need to be aware of how to obviate, by educational means, how even to preclude, such disorders. This latter idea might be thought of as a "health"-oriented idea rather than "disease"-oriented, as may be said of the other point of view.

The foregoing characterizes the kind of difference in attitude toward which we are striving in what is referred to as Epoch B as compared to Epoch A. Epoch B seems to be what might be called pro-life- and pro-health-oriented while in Epoch A the orientation seems to have been more anti-death and anti-disease. Obviously, attention must be given to both, from the viewpoint of survival and evolution. There is a considerable difference in a balanced view, compared to one in which there is a preponderant preoccupation with death and disease. Such an attitude was to be expected under circumstances in which disease and death predominated and survival of the species depended upon individual fertility and fecundity. Thus the greatest wish was for fertility and for warding off disease and death. Death was looked upon as a continuation of life, with the fulfillment of desire occurring in another world, another life, or another incarnation. The idea of the fulfillment of the BEING in this life seemed so unlikely that its expectations and hopes were deferred to a later time when it was imagined conditions would be more favorable.

In a period in which fertility (or its excessive effects) becomes disadvantageous, a new attitude toward the life of the individual develops. Less preoccupied by the possibility of his own early demise, it is understandable that a preoccupation with health for each individual will develop that he may be able to live a full and contributing life and not become a burden, to his own BEING and to others. In countries in which life expectancy has been increased by a reduction in the mortality rates of the young, more and more emphasis has fallen upon the maintenance of life of the older members of the population. Corresponding rearrangements in the roles and responsibilities prevailing in Epoch A have taken place. At present, the problem is one not merely of controlling disease and premature death but of controlling births and enhancing the value of longevity.

XV

COSMIC
PERSPECTIVE

An important distinction between the present and the past is to be noted in the greater prevalence today of individuals who are seeking, sensing, and expressing their own BEING. This statement might well be challenged because men at all times have expressed their dreams and fantasies. But there is a difference between today and the past in the diminution or weakening of external restraining influences such as existed in Epoch A, when authority over the individual was held by powerfully restrictive conventions of belief and behavior. Under such circumstances the BEING of Man was expressed extravagantly and beautifully by privileged élites as in the ancient cultures of China, Egypt, Greece, and Rome, and in more recent times in France, Spain, England, Germany, and Italy. Now, with authority and power in the modern world becoming more widely disseminated, there is a new need to learn how to exercise self-restraint in a disciplined way as well as to provide opportunities for self-expression of the BEING among larger and larger masses of people. The danger in the new circumstances lies in the increased difficulty in dealing with pathological individuals, groups, and movements against which defenses of a general kind are needed. Otherwise each individual would have to develop his own system of defense against those who do not possess self-restraining influences for their own BEING. This, clearly, is impossible. Thus society must develop new systems for identifying and dealing with those who were heretofore regarded as criminal and are now regarded as pathological.

Thus, in the course of the changes within a still relatively new culture such as that of the United States, which has gone through the stages of development described in the diagrams contained in the earlier chapters, we see the sequence through which I believe Man may also go in other parts of the world, with modifications attributable to local conditions. However, in cultures in which self-discipline has been strongly emphasized, from early life on, self-expression will, perhaps, be possible in a more balanced and perhaps even more satisfactory way than under circumstances in which external restraints have been removed without the concomitant development of self-restraint. Regardless of the form in which this occurs, it would seem reasonable to assume that the metabiological development and evolution of Man, with fuller expression of the individual BEING, will occur as external restraints permit. For this there is need of an internal system of restraints through the balanced development of the BEING and EGO systems, to produce a disciplined effect.

For a long time it was thought that the earth was flat, that the sun revolved around it, that Man was specially created apart from other living organisms. When Man first realized that the earth was round and revolved around the sun, it was not because of a change in the earth or the sun or in their relationship to each other but rather because of a change of his own perception of these objects and relationships. Now something new is taking place in man's relationship to Man and to the species which is more than conceptual; it is revealed in the shift from Epoch A to Epoch B, as a result of which Man's concept of his own BEING and EGO, and his relation to others, will have to evolve in a way appropriate to these altered circumstances. Whereas the change in Man's concept of his relationship to the earth and the sun was influenced by increasing scientific knowledge, the present change to which I am referring is due to an actual shift in relationships and not merely to a change in Man's conceptual understanding of his world. These conceptual relationships are shown in Figure 21, in which the

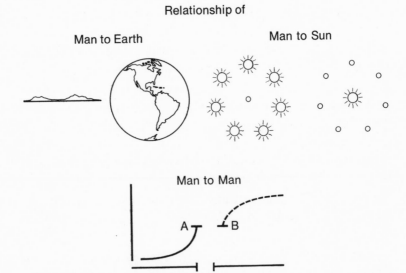

Figure 21. The upper left pair of symbols refers to the change in man's concept of the earth from flat to round; the upper right set refers to man's earlier concept of the sun revolving around the earth, which gave way to his notion that the earth revolved around the sun. The lower set of curves suggests man's earlier condition, described by Curve A, and his presently developing state as suggested by the shape of Curve B.

following are depicted: Man's changed view of the shape of the earth from flat to round; Man's changed view of the relationship of the earth to the sun relative to the rotation of one around the other; and, finally, Man's changing relationship to himself in the transition from Epoch A to Epoch B. The difference in perception and in behavior required by the change from Epoch A to Epoch B is as revolutionary, in its way, as the other major alterations in orientation experienced in the past.

Another way of seeing where Man is in cosmic evolution at this point in time is shown in Figure 22. This chart depicts

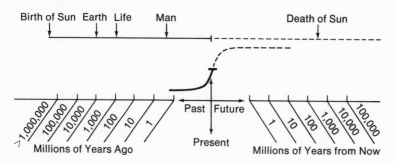

Figure 22

the sun as having been born millions of millions of years ago; it is estimated that it will die about 5,000 million years from now. It is estimated that the earth came into existence approximately 10,000 million years ago and life as having begun about 2,000 million years ago; Man emerged about 3 million years ago and is now at a very important nodal point in this evolutionary process—at the juncture between a qualitatively different past and future as suggested by the sigmoid curve marked at its point of inflection. At the present time Man is being tested for attributes needed for solution of the problems arising from so major a change in circumstances as here depicted. The attribute of greatest importance may be wisdom, and in time we will be able to make this judgment. However, *wisdom implies making judgments in advance rather than retrospectively, and this is the test which Man now faces.* It requires that he become conscious of both his own evolutionary "agenda" and that of Nature's and that he modify his own to fit Nature's since experience dictates the futility of doing otherwise.

For this, he will have to learn how to join feeling and reason, nonverbal and verbal, as well as subjective and objective sources of information and problem-solving. Man's and Nature's agenda will become apparent to those able to link feeling and reason, and the other pairs of attributes of the mind that have been enumerated. In this way wholeness is achieved and maintained in both art and science, united as attributes of the metabiological aspects of Man each capable of contributing to solving problems in his life. These problems may be thought of as concerned with being and becoming, for the solution of which the methods of the scientist *and* the artist are required.

It is clear that the prevailing attitude of separateness in Epoch A must give way, in Epoch B, to the kind of inter-relationship evident in the intertwining depicted in the diagram (Figure 16, page 58). Moreover, it is likely that there is great need for those capable of functioning as artist *and* as scientist. This implies the ability to use those metabiologic attributes more heavily drawn upon by artists as well as those more heavily drawn upon by scientists. In due course, more and more individuals of the human species should be educated to be able to use the two sets of faculties to the fullest of their possibilities. While this establishes a high level of expectation, it should not be construed as demanding more than is biologically or metabiologically possible. It is meant to imply that fullness of health depends on Man's ability to use those powers to the extent to which he is capable. If such a state can be realized, it is to be anticipated that there will be a corresponding reduction in incidence of diseases attributable to maldevelopment or malfunctioning of the metabiologic systems. Because of the perpetuating effect of the causative factors from one generation to the next and of one individual, or group, upon another, it is even to be anticipated that an improvement in the incidence of metabiological equilibrium will have a disproportionately greater positive effect upon the health of Man, now and in the future.

Thus the necessity for a drastic change in value system comes to stage center as never before in human history. The diagrams suggest not only the need but an opportunity; they also suggest the problems and their difficulties. They reveal the magnitude of what is required of Man in the use of his unconscious as well as his conscious forces to influence his own individual life. The complexity of this problem matches its importance and must be examined to see if it can be subdivided into manageable compartments without being taken out of context, or out of contact with the whole.

XVI

TO BEHAVE
"AS IF"

ONE OF MAN'S GREATEST STRIVINGS is to reach into the
unknown. The as yet unseen draws him. We are trying to find
a way into the unrevealed inside of Man—to discover, if
possible, the hidden agenda that his life will eventually unfold. In the course of doing so, we hope to learn the nature
of this agenda, how it functions, and how we can conform to
it or change it.

The blindness of Man in this respect is reflected in the
presence of wisdom in relatively few. Many wise individuals
have had no formal education and yet behave judiciously.
They possess a powerful intuitive faculty and are able to
learn from experience, from what they observe. They draw
valid inferences from the available data, and use them
relevantly. Those who are so endowed are wise in proportion
to their capacity for enhancing their native faculties, which,
if present and exercised, can, in time and under appropriate
circumstances, become more and more effective. If wisdom
is needed for maintaining life now and in the future, those
who are less gifted need something more than they possess.

If wisdom is required now, as physical fitness once was, to endure during the transition from Epoch A to Epoch B and for survival in Epoch B, and if it is seen as a matter of practical importance, thought must be given to methods for enhancing and encouraging its growth, for establishing a basis upon which men will behave "as if" they were so endowed. The development of an appropriate ethic to serve in this way, regardless of the different forms in which it might be practiced, could become an activity in which all could engage. Debate as to what is the sensible thing to do would evoke views and positions which would reveal the different ways, of which we may not have been aware, that Man has for seeking wisdom and arriving at what is called truth. If wisdom and truth are related, then we must know the way to both, whether intuitive or cognitive; belief, knowledge, and truth must not be confused—each must be used appropriately.

Nature plays its game in which survival goes to the "fittest," the "best fit"; for Man, in addition to this, the development of wisdom, or acting as if he were sagacious, could become a game through which he could reach fulfillment. Such a challenge for Epoch B could give purpose to all interested in playing the game of life *for what can be given to it and received from it, not for how much can be taken and how little can be given.* It could be played by the wise and the unwise and help develop the skills of those who have a desire to win for the reward of satisfaction and fulfillment in the course of one's lifetime. The wise will measure and tend to give in the short term, to obtain gain in the long term. The unwise tend to take now but will likely lose later. But can the wise allow the unwise to do so for all, or for themselves alone? Who are they? What must they do? How can they discover themselves and others with whom to work? What can they do together? How are they going to act with the others? How might one deal with those who prefer to be unwise? Can we choose which we will be, when, and for how long? Can the world of the future be maintained for both? Is this not the way it has been? Is not wisdom a basis for selection among men, and is it not the ideal toward which some men have always aspired?

Even though the future always remains veiled, it is possible, nevertheless, to foresee enough now to suggest that if good sense does not prevail, human life will become more of a punishment than a rewarding experience. For protection against further degradation in the quality of life it will be necessary to augment and teach wisdom and truth, to establish a system of respect in the absence of the universal love that has failed to develop. Love remains desirable, mysterious, and attainable only under circumstances not yet controllable. Respect, however, even in the absence of love, can be developed, to serve the need for relationship and to fulfill the necessary purposes *of* life and purposes *in* life. Respect, even though often existing without known or conscious reasons, can be learned. For this, Man's cognitive and intuitive processes are *both* needed if wisdom and respect are to be used to help Mankind become a healthily functioning organism of complementarily and therefore interdependently related autonomous individuals.

Toward these ends talent, research and resources are needed to develop ways and means as well as skill in behaving as if Man were wise. A hierarchy will always exist of the immature, the not-yet-wise and the unwise, as well as those who possess the natural capacity to develop and express practical wisdom. To accomplish the latter has long been the aim of many men. Now a renewed effort is imperative not morally but rather by necessity, not only on the part of educators, other interested groups, foundations and governments, but on the part of all of us individually.

CONCLUSION:
WISDOM—
A NEW KIND
OF FITNESS

THE PURPOSE of this inquiry has been to extract concepts about Man drawn from an analysis of his behavior at this point in time, in an attempt to identify possible alternatives in the future based upon a number of assumptions, hypotheses, and facts.

It is clear that Man's biological evolution has proceeded and continues to proceed slowly through the process of mutation and natural selection locked in a well-guarded genetic-somatic mechanism. His metabiologic evolution, however, is more easily influenced and accelerated. This has occurred because of the impact upon his EGO and BEING of the development and evolution of his knowledge affecting his view of Nature, himself, and the relationship between the two. These effects, together with the advances and applications of technology, for which he is responsible, so modify him as to bring about still further changes in an endless sequence. To modulate either the processes of Nature or his own activities, or, at least, his response to them, he must understand that he is himself the cause of both the progress and the problems with which he must cope in his daily existence and in his developing future.

In a sense, Man is like the Frankenstein monster. He has been produced by the process of evolution itself, to which he now contributes actively. Constructed for fitness to survive under previously prevailing circumstances, he must now accommodate to new conditions of life that are radically different quantitatively and qualitatively, for which he is, in part, responsible. Through the evolutionary processes that have produced him, Man and Nature together are now, in effect, the joint authors of the human predicament.

Attributes and habits develop in the course of life as necessities for survival. Those culturally formed and induced early understandably persist as long as do the conditions that evoked them. However, they often tend to remain active even in the absence of the provoking conditions. This is true even of those based upon erroneous and no-longer-tenable perceptions, harmful prejudices, and unreasonable intolerances. They are also the cause of internal and external conflicts, and aggressive-defensive responses, that result in pathology (psychologically and sociologically) for which prevention or cure is required. Attitudes and reaction patterns thus established give the impression of being an ineradicable part of the individual and the species. Thus Man himself possesses the potential to cause many of his disorders as well as the attributes to develop means for their prevention and cure. This duality is revealed in many of the paradoxes of human life and is seen in living systems generally.

According to the criterion of fecundation, in which only members of the same species can reproduce, Man is a single species biologically. Differences of a metabiological nature, however, make it appear as if mankind were composed of many "species," or varieties, each of which regards the others with suspicion or hostility. Although some of the differences involved simply express the inherently complementary nature of the still-evolving human ecosystem, or of the elements, or parts, of the organism of mankind, they, too, often give rise to many of the unreasonable, and therefore unnecessary, conflicts with which Man lives. To help our understanding of man's relationship to Man, and Man's relationship to Nature, in terms of their inherent complementary character, analogies have been drawn between the "games" of Nature and of Man. The point that has already been made is that the laws that govern Nature's game require, under certain circumstances, "double-win" rather than "win-lose" resolutions which Man must also develop.

Although each of us would like to be "winners," at least in terms of individual satisfaction and fulfillment, it is also clear that more luck, knowledge, and wisdom are required than are possessed by very many. Some are more fortunate than others, but none are born either fully knowledgeable or infinitely wise; hence Man's search for perspective and guidance in dealing with the unknowns and uncertainties of life in all its complexity.

Since many of the problems for which Man seeks solution are an inherent part of the process of human development itself, and since he is both a contributing cause as well as a sufferer, his position as both patient and physician is a difficult one. And yet he must be both. Fortunately, means do exist for self-correction, for self-cure, and for prevention even of those potentially harmful or lethal effects which are self-induced. The approach employed here in thinking about this dilemma has been to seek useful analogies in the self-correcting processes that are an essential and integral part of living systems.

The assumption is that if individual man were aware of the existence of such processes and the way they operate, knowing that they are an integral part of his own self as well, he might develop the desire to learn how to use them consciously and deliberately not only for survival but for fulfillment in his lifetime. Such clues can be found in the way in which control and regulation operate in living Nature, where success is evidenced in the persistence of life in spite of vicissitudes, difficulties, and seeming impossibilities. On the assumption that metabiologic evolutionary problems are similar to problems encountered and solved in biological evolution, analogies are sought to serve as models helping us to deal more realistically, and therefore more appropriately, with some of our unresolved problems, and, even, possibly to accept the existence of insoluble enigmas.

Referring to Man as a metabiological entity infers that he possesses self-correcting, self-controlling, and self-disciplining mechanisms, as well as biologically governed balance-mechanisms for each of his two distinct yet related evolutionary purposes, i.e., for improving the quality of life as well as for survival. It implies, also, that change in human behavior which will serve both biological and metabiological aims requires many steps and stages involving both error-making and error-correcting. In spite of our prior limitations, due to ignorance of the character or details of the processes involved in evolution, can we, now, with our increased knowledge of the nature of living systems, and of Man, apply ourselves to conceive of ways and means of influencing the course of future events toward fulfilling Man's evolutionary potential? In Epoch A it appears that greater success has been achieved in reducing premature death than in improving the quality of life in terms of individual satisfaction. Hence, to the gains made in Epoch A, facilitating survival by better hygienic conditions and other measures for the prevention of disease, new challenges will have to be accepted in Epoch B, testing Man's ingenuity in developing the means to enhance the degree of fulfillment in the life of the individual and in the quality of life generally.

The difficulties and complexities involved in such a challenge are considerable; the mere existence of innate mechanisms for meeting them does not mean that the odds are in favor of success. Human history is replete with evidence that *de*volutionary processes also operate, with deterioration of the human condition, unless foresight, imagination, ingenuity, determination, and wisdom are brought to bear, to increase self-awareness and self-discipline in the choice of ends as well as means. To be able to prevent such deterioration, principles will be required by which to live, and by which to intervene judiciously in the process of biologic and metabiologic evolution with knowledge of the *de*volutionary as well as the evolutionary consequences of each action or nonaction when we face issues which affect our well-being individually and collectively.

The hypothesis has been proposed that if the mind of Man is exposed to the economy of Nature, as revealed in the workings of living systems, he will become sensitized to recognize the necessity of balancing values. Thus measure is established as the source of wisdom. By improving the quality of life, wisdom, thus, can influence the processes of metabiological evolution, just as the enhancement of physical fitness functioned in the struggle for survival in biological evolution. If Man can come to recognize that the use of wisdom in the game of life leads to the reward of a greater measure of fulfillment and satisfaction, then he will value the development of such special skills; nowadays more individuals have the opportunity to do so for more years than was generally true heretofore. In this, everyone has much to gain.

If, in the course of this quest, a struggle arises between the wise and the nonwise, the conquest or elimination of either one would result in loss to both, just as if Life and Death were to "conquer or eliminate" each other. The wise must avoid a "win-lose" conflict with the unwise, just as it was necessary in biological evolution for Life and Death to arrive at a "double-win" resolution in order for either one, and hence both, to persist. Even though Death eventually wins over Life so far as the individual is concerned, Life wins over Death in the perpetuation of the species. This is to say that Life "wins immortality" for the species and Death, mortality for the individual; the individual may be unwise, but not the species. For the quality of life to be improved, and for survival, Mankind will have to respect those who are wise and expect the individual to behave as if he were. If wisdom is, in fact, a new kind of fitness for survival, the operation of the equivalent of natural selection in the metabiological evolutionary processes will have been guided by the choice of human values.

In Epoch A Man acted effectively on the side of Life, both of the individual and of the species, by reducing the incidence of disease and the frequency of dying prematurely. Correspondingly, in Epoch B Man may be able to devise ways of improving the quality of life of the individual and of the species by reducing unwisdom or its adverse effects and by respecting and applying wisdom for increasing the possibility of personal fulfillment. Among individuals who now have less to struggle for personally in order to survive, as a result of the changes brought about in Epoch A, a new syndrome has developed, manifest in seeming purposelessness, for the treatment of which new experiences will be needed, possibly leading to new motivations.

Judgment is required in larger measure than ever before if Man is to succeed in balancing the adverse effects, both upon the species and upon individuals, resulting from the increased knowledge and improved technology that reduce the need for struggle and also the opportunity to learn how to experience a sense of satisfaction. This is seen among the increasing numbers of individuals whose lives have been prolonged and made more secure by the metabiological evolutionary developments that have occurred in recent times, without effort on their part.

There is a further undesirable side effect of the benefits brought about in Epoch A. Among the individuals who feel purposeless, some become wantonly and pathologically destructive, threatening and interfering with the development and achievement of fulfillment of others. For resolving such problems as these, far more insight is needed than has as yet been activated.

By suggesting the idea of survival of the wisest I mean not only that the more discerning will survive but also that the survival of Man, with a life of high quality, depends upon the prevalence of respect for wisdom and for those possessing a sense of the BEING of Man and of the laws of Nature. These are necessary for choosing from among alternatives, for fulfillment as well as for survival. Man's metabiological questions and problems still need answers. For this a great deal more understanding is required through the development of an approach similar to the unraveling of the details of the relationship between structure and function in biological systems. The idea of wisdom as a pro-health, pro-life, pro-evolutionary influence still leaves open and unresolved the question as to how this might be developed and applied. Man's capacity to bring this about is also not known. The role of religious and political organizations has been to enlighten and to guide. Now new means are needed for inner self-regulation based upon naturalistic rather than on arbitrary moralistic formulations. In spite of the difficulties involved in devising and developing such formulations, this could provide an important purpose *in* life and serve the purpose *of* life individually and collectively.

The extent reached by Man in his capacity to create, to destroy, and to move in space as well as over the surface of the earth has indeed been remarkable. To what extent does he have the ability to invent new ways to act wisely as a species even if his aptitude to so behave individually is relatively limited?

Exposing Man's mind to the laws of Nature may help him discover and apply whatever insight and foresight he possesses for dealing with the problems of relationships to himself and to others, and to the universe. This way of thinking about Man and Nature and relationship and wisdom is new to most, and to be of value will require modern patterns of perceiving one's self and others. New attitudes and behavioral patterns will follow.

It is simpler to conceive such notions than to apply them in everyday life. Nevertheless, it is far easier to reach objectives based upon sound concepts and hypotheses than upon those without basis. Hence the challenge with which Man is generally confronted at this point is to see himself as a biological and metabiological entity, possessing attributes capable of reversing some of the *de*volutionary trends. These attributes can also be directed and disciplined to facilitate and increase the probability of achieving a greater measure of fulfillment in life than has been possible until now.

Paradoxically, this challenge and hope exist in the face of enigmas more difficult to overcome than ever before, because greater opportunities for fulfillment are matched by correspondingly greater obstacles. For this reason, wisdom, understood as a new kind of strength, is a paramount necessity for Man. Now, even more than ever before, it is required as a basis for fitness, to maintain life itself on the face of this planet, and as an alternative to paths toward alienation or despair.

ABOUT THE AUTHOR

JONAS SALK is presently Director and Fellow of the
Salk Institute for Biological Studies in La Jolla, California. He is also an Adjunct Professor in the Health
Sciences at the University of California, San Diego.
The Institute for Biological Studies, which he founded,
is dedicated not only to experimental biology but to
relating biological knowledge to philosophical, psychological, and social questions. Dr. Salk views biology
not only as a science but as a basic cultural discipline
with unifying potential for the relationships that exist
between man and the physical universe, as well as
between man and the sciences, arts, and humanities.
His first book, *Man Unfolding*, was also published by
Harper & Row.

4. Dealing with problems of life or pass to
the problem process of life.

73 74 75 10 9 8 7 6 5 4 3 2 1